The

HELPING YOUR KIDS DO

Relaxed

MORE AS YOU DO LESS

Parent

The

HELPING YOUR KIDS DO

Relaxed

MORE AS YOU DO LESS

Parent

Tim Smith

NORTHFIELD PUBLISHING
CHICAGO

ISBN: 1-881273-60-1

3 5 7 9 10 8 6 4

Printed in the United States of America

to
Suzanne

Flowers, friends,
and children
Are more beautiful
Because of
Your graceful touch.

CONTENTS

Acknowledgments   9
Introduction: How to Run the Parenting Perennial   11
1. Parenting Fantasies   15
2. *Suave Con Estilo*   27
3. Parenting in Reality   37
4. Hurried, Hassled, and Hushed   49
5. Princes and Princesses   65
6. Spoiled-Rotten Kids   77
7. The Forty-Year-Old Adolescent   91
8. From Generation to Generation   103
9. The Relaxed Relationship   119
10. The Relaxed Conversation   133
11. How to Motivate Your Kids   149
12. Teaching Response-ability   165
13. Remote-Control Parenting   179
14. Teaching Your Children Well   195
15. Becoming the Relaxed Parent   209
Notes   219

The Fourteen Parenting Principles
of the Relaxed Parent

1. The relaxed parent accepts parenting truths and rejects parenting myths.
2. The relaxed parent balances rules with relationship.
3. The relaxed parent has realistic expectations—of himself and of his children.
4. The relaxed parent understands the trends affecting children in order to understand his own children.
5. The relaxed parent prepares his children for life by treating them as family members, not guests.
6. The relaxed parent chooses to not give children too much, recognizing to do so may be giving them too little.
7. The relaxed parent anticipates the changes of each stage of life, and prepares himself and his children for each one.
8. The relaxed parent carefully evaluates what he has inherited before passing it on to his children.
9. The relaxed parent seeks to strengthen the relationship with his children, because he understands that not every moment is a teachable moment.
10. The relaxed parent realizes effective communication with children differs from effective communication with adults.
11. The relaxed parent has developed a strategy to move from bribing to motivating.
12. The relaxed parent turns over areas of response-ability to his children to help them learn from the consequences.
13. The relaxed parent guides his children by moving from a position of control to a position of influence.
14. Relaxed parents guide their children with timeless principles based on universal truth, not with the latest formulas.

ACKNOWLEDGMENTS

I keep busy writing, speaking, and working with families. Sometimes I get on my horse and ride off in six directions. But there is always a faithful guide to point me in the right direction, water the horse, or remind me to pace myself. She is always equipped, willing, and capable. But best of all, she is *relaxed!* Without her as my trusty administrative assistant, I'd be lost and horseless. Thanks, Patti Schultz, for being both a friend and coworker.

I also appreciate the support I received from Jim Bell, editorial director at Northfield Publishing. His enthusiasm for a practical and fun-to-read parenting book has greatly motivated me.

Parenting is a challenge. It requires energy and experience. Anything worthwhile demands something of us. Being a parent demands that I grow. I am grateful for the lessons I have learned and am learning from our daughters, Nicole and Brooke. Thanks to both of you! Because of you I had the inspiration to write this book. Because of you I saw the need to write this book! Now, watch me and see if I really am *The Relaxed Parent.*

INTRODUCTION

HOW TO RUN
THE PARENTING PERENNIAL

*C*ould you bring me another lemonade?" I ask from my hammock, strung between two gently swaying palm trees.

"Would you like a chocolate chip cookie with that, Dad? I just baked some. They have macadamia nuts. They are your favorite."

"Why sure, Brooke, that would be great."

"Here you are, Father. I'll check on you later, after I finish cleaning the house. Nicole is washing the cars; earlier we mowed the lawn. Oh, by the way, would you like something to read? Here is your favorite magazine that just came in the mail. My report card came too. Here, take a look," my daughter says proudly.

"All A's! That's wonderful!"

"Yeah, it looks like I'll get that college scholarship after all. Don't you worry about paying for college, Daddy. Just relax and enjoy yourself."

It's an enjoyable fantasy, isn't it? Is it possible? It seems like an oxymoron: relaxed and parent. Can the two words legally be placed side by side? I mean, in most cases fresh-baked cookies and volunteer house cleanings seem a sign of a midday reverie or an impending request for a bigger allowance or a ride somewhere. More often we can expect, depending on our child's age, dirty diapers, crying, dirty bedrooms, whining, dirty clothes, or arguments over bedtime, boyfriends, or borrowing the car keys. This does not seem like the formula for staying relaxed.

Certainly it was easier to be relaxed before you had kids. Once your first child was born, you became a runner in the world's longest marathon: the Parenting Perennial. In all likelihood, you began with a surge of energy and hopeful dreams. But before too long your pace began to slacken. You realized you went out too fast.

That's what this book is about, finishing the Parenting Perennial and running relaxed in the process. I suspect you're now weary in the race. A loss of sleep and the weight training of lugging baby stuff has taken its toll. You may be at the wall called Teen Years, an obstacle much higher than you imagined. And, now, in the midst of the race, you realize the course description never mentioned the steep hills, hidden ruts, and this thick wall awaiting as you continue along the Parenting Perennial. Maybe your legs are burning from the pain, and the sweat has dripped into your eyes, causing them to sting and blur.

The goal of *The Relaxed Parent* is to help you run well and to actually finish feeling good about what's happened. In a marathon, runners often feel like quitting. They may force themselves to jog on, but they have help along the way. At different points, they can see the goal, slow for refreshment, whether Gatorade® drink or simple water, and receive shouts of: "Keep going, you're doing great!" The shouts of the spectators can renew a runner's passion to finish the race well.

I believe *The Relaxed Parent* will provide all three aids: a view of the goal, a pause that refreshes, and encouragement along the way. I want to give you stamina in your parenting. I want to revitalize you in the parenting marathon, with humor, advice, and the shouts of encouragement. "Keep going! You are doing fine."

The two main pieces of advice from Coach Smith are: "Relax your breathing" and "Keep up the pace." Being relaxed about yourself and your children is very important, as we shall see. And pacing is key to marathon runners and parents alike.

The relaxed parent has a sense of pace. She knows that parenting is not a sprint; it's a marathon. To finish the race well, you need to run relaxed. That is the goal of *The Relaxed Parent*, to offer you coaching to help you run relaxed.

One of the first things we'll discover is *helping your kids do more as you do less*. Sounds great, doesn't it? Is it possible? I think so. But it depends on your child's motivation. We will discuss how to motivate our children.

Do you ever worry about your children when they are away from you? When they are out of town—or twenty feet away in their bedroom/fortress? We will look at an anxiety-releasing approach I call *remote-control parenting* (chapter 13). We'll take a look at ourselves as we consider the concept of *the forty-year-old adolescent* (chapter 7).

To help us find the way, I introduce one principle per chapter for becoming the relaxed parent. (You'll find these listed together on page 8.) In addition, each chapter concludes with "Reflections for the Relaxed Parent," questions for you to think about or discuss with friends. Take some time to reflect on these. Talking about these items with your mate or friends can give you even more perspective.

Following "Reflections" is the "Skill Builder," a practical action step for you to apply the principle presented in the chapter. Learning to be the relaxed parent does require some preparation. These Skill Builder exercises will get you started in developing the skills needed for relaxed parenting.

This book isn't about being the perfect parent. It's about being relaxed and realistic. I have declared these pages to be a guilt-free zone. I don't want our focus to be on what we *should* have done as parents, but on what we *can* do. That is why I offer fifty-two ideas on what to say and do to become the relaxed parent. (For those of you who like to read the introduction and the last chapter before you buy a book, turn to page 212 for the fifty-two ideas.)

With two daughters of my own, I'm with you in the race. Hope you enjoy the views along the way, and happy jogging!

$\mathcal{P}$ARENTING $\mathcal{P}$RINCIPLE

*The relaxed parent accepts parenting
truths and rejects parenting myths.*

ONE

PARENTING FANTASIES

I have a parenting fantasy. I want to be Cliff Huxtable, that happy and wise father of the hit TV program, "The Cosby Show." The setting may change, but the outcome of the fantasy is always the same: Father knows best. My fantasy, as Cliff, goes something like this:

"Theo, you crashed the car into the living room of our luxurious townhouse. But the important point is that you learned a lesson. I'm sure next time you'll handle the situation differently," says Dad in his multicolored designer sweater.

"Dad, I'm sorry. I just wanted to impress Shautrice. You know, she's a babe! I forgot which pedal was the brake."

"Son, I'm glad we could have this talk. Women and cars can be a dangerous combination. Those hormones can easily distract you. But there will have to be a consequence for your behavior. You may not borrow my Mercedes for a month. If you need a car, you'll just have to settle for your own Acura. Do you understand?"

"Yeah . . . sure, Dad," the son responds dejectedly.

"You have had a tough night, Son. Let's head into the kitchen for a Pudding Pop®."

That's my parenting fantasy. Like all good TV parents, I can resolve crises and have time for a snack within twenty-four minutes.

If only real-life parenting were like that, right?

One reason I fantasize about being a parent like Cliff Huxtable is because he always seemed to be home. Didn't that guy ever work? I like the idea of lounging around a luxury home in expensive sweaters, snacking, and cracking jokes. Let the wife work. Just hang out and be the perfect parent. Not overreacting. Not yelling. Not stressed about finances. Just the cool, relational, in-control dad. It's a wonderful fantasy!

My parenting experience is about as opposite to Cliff Huxtable's as it could be.

I have to work, so I don't get to lounge around the house. Our house is the size of the Huxtable's master bedroom.

I'm not cool like Cliff Huxtable. I tend to jump in with my mouth and overreact. My kids push my buttons and I definitely don't look cool and in control. Even if I'm wearing my new sweater from Penney's.

It has been my experience that parenting is a lot like sports: "The thrill of victory, and the agony of defeat." It's definitely a mixed bag. Unless you're on TV.

I am encouraged, though. In my exhaustive research (I read a magazine article in the dentist's office) I discovered that many parents enjoy fantasies like mine. We all need a delightful escape from the realities of the drudgery of parenting.

The downside (and there always seems to be one in parenting) is that sooner or later we have to stop fantasizing, take out the trash, and get back to reality.

I wish we could live in Fantasy Land. But sooner than later, our kids force reality in our face. *Pooof!* and the magic bubble of illusion is burst. My dreams of being like Cliff come crashing down when my kids threaten to kill each other over the remote control.

As parents, you and I must deal with unmet expectations. We are forced to deal with disappointment. One reason we are not always relaxed parents is because we sometimes buy into the myth of how parenting actually progresses—a hitch here, a miss there, but no repeating disappointments. For both parents and their children, there are expectations, and so there are disappointments. My visit with Greg (not his real name) a few years ago reminded me of this truth.

"My son is disappointed in me," Greg confessed as he stared dejectedly into his coffee. "I just don't know what to do. It seems like we are drifting apart. I'm anxious that I'm not doing what I should be doing. But I don't know what he wants. He will graduate and be gone in eight months. I know he is disappointed. What does he want?"

WHAT OUR CHILDREN WANT FROM US

I had a difficult time believing the words I was hearing. Greg is a well-known community leader and professional in his field. He has wealth, fame, and influence. But at this breakfast, he was perplexed and defeated.

"What do kids want?" he asked again.

I began trying to answer Greg's question, which was really a plea to understand his boy. "Recently I had the opportunity to speak to a large group of high school students at a camp. I asked them this same question, 'What do you want from your parents?' One of the first responses was 'Cash!' Another was 'No curfew!' But I did get some serious responses. And I have seen these affirmed in my counseling kids for the last twenty years. Do you want to know what these six hundred kids said were the top three things they want from their parents?"

"Sure!" the father said with anticipation.

"Kids want our care, our time, and for us to be real. It seems that these are three crucial needs for a healthy parent-child relationship. At least from the kids' viewpoint."

"Care, time, and authenticity," repeated the father.

"If these are the three truths about kids, it might be helpful to consider their opposites. You know, three myths about kids," I told Greg. "If we understand these myths, we can avoid them and build our relationship with our kids on truth. When we build our expectations of our kids on myths, we sow seeds of rebellion and alienation."

"Are you saying that I may have been entertaining some false ideas about my son, and this has led to his disappointment?"

I took the risk to be truthful. "Yes, I think that's what has happened. Myths seem right because they are familiar. But famil-

iarity does not equal authenticity. Myths may seem harmless at
first; but with a deeper look, we discover that they can become
barriers in our relationship with our child. If your child is disappointed in you it might be because you have ignored these three
truths about kids and believed a myth."

"What do you think I could do to show my son I want to
change from myths to reality? How can I get him to not be disappointed in me or mad at me?"

"You might try taking him out to breakfast once a week and
just talking. Get to know each other as men. Share your struggles, worries, and victories. You only have a few months to build
a relationship that could last a lifetime."

"Wow! That's such a simple but great idea. That way I can
show care, spend time, and be authentic all at one time. I don't
know why I didn't think of that."

I don't either, I thought.

THREE TRUTHS—AND THREE
MYTHS—ABOUT OUR KIDS' NEEDS

What kept this father from understanding three basic truths
about his teenage son? I think it might have been his mindset. I
think that his perspective was more influenced by myths than
truth. Maybe he thought he was Ward Cleaver. I do know many
parents accept the myths. But relaxed parents will rear their children based on truths about children. Knowing the truth frees us
to focus on what is helpful for our kids. So, as we begin our journey to becoming relaxed parents, here are three truths about the
needs our children have as well as the myths that get in the way
of our meeting those needs.

Truth #1: "Kids Need Our Care"

Kids need our help, and, despite an occasional protest, they
truly want it. Maybe you have accepted the myth that sometimes
obscures Truth #1. The myth says: *"Kids are resilient, they'll get
over it."* This myth implies that kids are somehow immune from

hurt. Divorcing parents and parents who are moving the family to a new area sometimes say that. So do parents who are unaware of (or unconcerned for) their child's feelings and pain.

Have you said or thought those words: The kids will get over it? The myth may seem somewhat true. After all, children don't respond in the same way that adults do to change and pain. The same things that trouble adults trouble kids—they just deal with them differently. Adults may show their worry by talking about something frequently. Kids may have the same worry but may choose to keep silent about it. But the truth is our children desire to have us show care for them, both by what we say and do.

A fifteen-year-old boy was so sad about being forced to move that he set the new house on fire. A seventeen-year-old girl seemed to be dealing well with her parents' divorce, and her mom even commented on how "resilient" she was. Three months later, she was smoking marijuana every day. When I asked her, "Where does it hurt?" she answered, "You are the first adult that understands my hurt."

Expecting our children to bounce back from loss is not only unrealistic, but cruel. Recovery from loss and pain takes time, understanding, and often guidance.

Our children will feel more valued if we demonstrate that we are aware of how the losses of life affect them. Expecting them to be resilient creates pressure to hurry up with their grief and "get over it."

Pretending that our kids are resilient demonstrates for them a very dangerous example: If you don't like reality, create your own. As they mature they may copy us, substituting a false, new "reality" for the real world.

This kind of pretending feeds a lot of craziness and substance abuse. If the pain is too great, most kids will look for a painkiller. Alcohol and drugs are effective, easy-access painkillers, available to most kids in our country. Talking about the pain is a much better approach than pretending it's not there.

Truth #2: "Kids Need Time with Us"

I handed the tissues to the sobbing sixteen-year-old in my office.

"I would give up what we have just to be with my dad more. All he does is work!"

Sharon cried, blew her nose, and continued, "What does it matter, the car, the boat, the house on the water? I mean, if I can't have time with him?"

I thought about the luxury car Sharon received for her sixteenth birthday. *A lot of kids would love to have a Mercedes to drive,* I thought. I also thought about the designer clothes that filled her walk-in closet; the exotic vacations she took with her mother; and the beautiful beach-front estate they lived in.

"You would trade in your wealth, just to be with your dad?"

"Well, maybe not all of it."

I didn't think so, I thought. *I'll take the Mercedes,* I even told myself.

"But I would live at a much lower standard of living just to spend more time with my dad before I go off to college. I'll be gone in a year and I want to get to know him better before I leave."

Sharon had an ache in her soul for her father. She loved him. She enjoyed spending time with him. She needed the security of a close relationship with him before she launched off into the uncertainty of college. To Sharon, a close relationship with her dad was more of a basic need than material wealth.

"Does your dad know how you feel?"

"No, I never have brought it up. Our time is so limited. I usually just smile and pretend everything is OK."

"How do you feel about telling him how you really feel?"

"I am scared to do that. What should I say?"

"Try something like this: 'Dad, I appreciate all the hard work you have put into your job, and all the nice things you have provided for me. Now, before I go off to college, I would like to spend more time together. It will help me prepare to go.'

"What do you think?" I asked.

"It's worth a try. He's home this weekend. I'll talk to him then."

Sharon talked to her father. He was surprised that she wanted to spend more time with him. He had always believed that teens don't want to spend time with their parents. He felt that providing nice things was his way of showing Sharon that he loved her. Sharon's dad had been deluded by the second myth: *"Our kids know we love them by all the hard work we put into our careers to provide for them."*

Parents sometimes think children associate taking care of their physical needs—food, shelter, and clothing—and a few conveniences, with love. Fathers are especially prone to this attitude. But the truth is, kids do not comprehend the equation:

Hard Work = Love.

More mothers are being forced to work outside the home; economic realities demand it. Many moms struggle with the same issues as Sharon's dad. They put in eight hours at work and come home to a mound of laundry, a sink of dirty dishes, and a child reposed on the couch, ready to ask, "What's for dinner?"

Kids don't understand that Mom's hard work is evidence of her love. Children are more relational. They appreciate relationships even more than adults, so they feel highly valued when we spend time with them. We need to show love by being with them. Though parents typically are more task-oriented than children (we place more value on "getting things done"), we must remember that our children prefer relationship to work. For them the equation reads:

Time Together = Love.

Have you ever asked your children three or four times to complete their chores? Most kids don't value work like their parents do. Many kids don't understand what we do at work, let alone understand that we work so hard because we love them and want to provide for them. (If you're a stay-at-home spouse, congratulations! Your time available for the children probably is greater than the time your working mate has. Try not to let the household tasks and the monotony of the sometimes-recurring routine lull you to putting your children onto auto-pilot, playing by themselves. They need your involvement, too.)

We can teach our kids the value of working hard and being diligent. But we should not expect that they will automatically perceive our work ethic as love for them.

This is an unrealistic expectation that will lead to disappointment.

Truth #3: "Kids Need Us to Be Authentic"

Our children want to see us as we really are. Accurate perceptions lead to freedom and clarity in relationships. When we are insincere about who we are, whether we hide our true feelings or act other than who we are, we tend to confuse our kids, which leads to barriers in relationships. Yet many parents tend to accept the following myth: *"Parents need to maintain a good image in front of their kids and others."*

Breaking loose of the third myth can be very liberating to parents. Our kids already know our weaknesses; they are waiting to see if we will admit to them. Some of you may be struggling with this idea, so let me ask you:

- Are there things your child does that really aggravate you?
- What does your child do that really pushes your buttons?
- Do you think they know your hot buttons?

Our children have been studying us for years; they are experts on nonverbal communication. They know how to read us. They know how to set us off. Kids are experts in manipulating their parents; it's a technical skill that they have refined. Children are students of their parents. As adults we must be careful. We tend to be more verbal and say things, things that may or may not be true. Children live in a more visual world; they watch for facial expressions, body language, tone of voice, and behavior. Their perceptions are often more accurate, regardless of what adults say. In one classic study by Albert Mehrabin (reported in his book *Silent Messages*), the Stanford University researcher demonstrated that "the loudest messages are nonverbal (especially with children): 55 percent of what we communicate consists of nonverbal messages sent through eye contact (or lack of eye contact), facial expressions, and body language; 38 percent is tone of voice (how we say what we say), and only 7 percent is content!"[1]

As I was writing this, Brooke, our eleven-year-old, came in with a complaint about her sister. She took one look at my face and said, "Never mind, Dad. I don't want to talk with you about her right now, not with that face."

"What face? What's wrong with my face?" I demanded.

"It's just a face that looks bothered, and you'll get mad at me for interrupting," she explained.

She was deadly accurate. I didn't even realize how annoyed I was with her until she simply shared her observation. In two seconds time she had precisely analyzed my emotions. She knows me because she has been studying me for eleven years.

All children are like this. They see our strengths as well as our foibles, they are looking to see how we use our strengths, and if we disguise our weaknesses. As parents, we can't hide our weaknesses from our kids, so why try?

Trying to maintain a good image in front of the kids only worked on "Leave It to Beaver." I've got news for you: Your kid isn't Beaver, and you aren't Ward or June. Join the real world where we don't have to create a facade about our family. Kids don't need heroes as much as they need authentic models to pattern their lives after. If they don't have models in their real world, they may be forced to settle for heroes in their imaginary world. Seek to be an example for your child by being real, not fake. When we are real, we increase the chances that our children will copy our behavior. We would be proud to have our children emulate our authenticity.

Maintaining a good image is not only difficult, it is impossible. Some of the most neurotic parents are the ones who have swallowed this myth. They live with the obsessive drive to be perfect. They live with the disappointing and destructive delusion that if they are perfect parents, they will have perfect kids.

Nothing sets us up for more disappointment than perfection. We need a realistic appraisal of our children and ourselves. We need the freedom to not be perfect, or have perfect children. If we have accurate perceptions, based on what *is,* rather than what we wish, we will have the freedom to realistically enjoy our relationships with our children.

Myths are the fog that encompasses our parent-child relationships and lead to disappointment. The fog rises out of our own unmet needs as parents. People, especially our own children, cannot make us feel good about ourselves. Forcing our needs on the next generation sets us all up for disappointment.

We should challenge our children to do their best and be their best; but it needs to be for *their* sakes. Children can never make up for what's lacking in us, and they should not have to.

When we are able to discuss real expectations and be reasonable with our children, we are on the road to preparing them for their journey in life. We also are taking the first step toward becoming a relaxed parent, for being realistic will let us stay relaxed. When we have a parenting perspective based on truth—knowing what our children need—we are on our way to becoming effective parents. We also will be able to say no to our children's unreasonable requests. Saying no will allow us to spend our energies on those things that are truly important for our children, while ignoring those things that our children unwisely request. In doing this, we will equip our children for the journey of life, including both the thrill of victory and the agony of defeat.

Reflections

FOR THE RELAXED PARENT

1. What TV program has the most unrealistic families? Most realistic?
2. Have you ever agreed with the myth, "Kids are resilient; they'll get over it"? What was the situation?
3. As children mature, how does time with them change?
4. What are some of the risks of being authentic with our children?
5. What are some ways parents can be authentic?
6. Where do we draw the line with our authenticity?
7. "Nothing sets us up for more disappointment than perfection." Do you agree with this statement?

Skill Builder

"CAT SCAN"

Take time to "CAT-scan" your parenting. Using the acrostic CAT, evaluate your parenting for Care, Authenticity, and Time.

C—How does my child need me to show *care*?
A—How can I be *authentic* with my child?
T—What would be some effective ways to spend *time* with my child?

Try to respond to each of these questions for each child. You'll probably discover different responses for different children, and at different times.

$\mathcal{P}$ARENTING
$\mathcal{P}$RINCIPLE

The relaxed parent balances
rules with relationship.

TWO

SUAVE
CON ESTILO

"*B*ueno hombre. Punto lindo!"

As I jogged back to midfield, my teammates patted and applauded me. I had just made a goal. "Good man. Pretty point!" was the translation. *Score one for the gringo*. I was feeling proud.

Maybe they will accept me. Being good at soccer is important in Honduras. I wanted to show them I could play. But down here, close to the equator, it wasn't just power soccer. An accomplished soccer player in Latin America has style, not just strength or speed.

I had demonstrated a little finesse with my goal. I put the move on the defense and kicked it. Surprisingly, it went in.

"Suave con estilo," said Luis with a cool smile.

"Suave con estilo," I repeated. Luis nodded his head with affirmation. *I was in! The locals would now accept me as a competent soccer player and cool guy!*

You see, Luis had just given me the ultimate compliment: "Suave con estilo."

It may not mean much to you, but it was huge to me. Roughly translated, it means "Smooth, with style," or "Cool, with style."

I wanted to be cool. I wanted to be accepted. I didn't want to be the "Ugly American." I wanted to be *suave con estilo*.

Being cool is a pretty important value, especially to a California surfer like me. But when it comes to parenting, "cool" is an oxymoron. I don't know what it is, but it's hard to look cool when you are a parent. It's like you trade in your cool when you pick up your baby at the hospital.

I can hear the nurse now. "Sir, your baby and wife are on the maternity ward. Stop off at the business office and turn in all your cool (and your cash) and then pick up your baby."

We adults spend so much time trying to be cool. Before I was married I used to hang out at discos, wearing my white Angel Flight double-knit polyester suit (with vest) and three-inch platform shoes. With the Afro, I was the epitome of cool. (This was several years ago, now.) I couldn't dance, but I *looked* cool.

As a young married guy, I still was kind of cool. Suzanne and I went out on dates. Ate dinner out four times a week. Bought trendy stuff. Went on cool weekend trips.

And then it happened!

We had a baby.

Kids are cool-suckers. I don't care where you live, how much money you have, or how hip you dress. You'll be exponentially less cool the longer you have kids. (Translation: "You are becoming a nerd.")

For example, pre-baby I drove a Triumph Spitfire sports car. Two-seater. Raspberry red. Completely restored. Deafening eight-track stereo.

With first baby, I drove a white Toyota Corolla. AM radio. No air-conditioning. Brown plastic seats.

My cool was withering.

Infant car seats rob any ground gained trying to look cool. Cruising down the California freeway, surfboard on the top— there's a baby seat in the back. I try to look hip as people blast by. But it's a feeble attempt.

Parents are destined to cool-anemia.

But that's OK.

Once you have kids, you realize that being cool was overrated. But deep down inside, we still want to be cool. We want people to pat us on the back and say, "Suave con estilo." "Smooth and styling."

How can we be parents and still be cool?

"Grace under pressure." That's what we want. Three-year-old Benjy is throwing a fit in the store. He's toppled the display of Power Morphin Ninja tennis shoes.

"I want Toxic Waste Glow-in-the-Dark green high tops! Not the purple ones!" shouts Benjy. Salespeople are raising eyebrows. Customers pause and gawk.

A tense moment. *What will you do?* Your authority has been challenged by a thirty-four pounder.

How can you be the relaxed parent? How can you be cool?

YOUR PARENTING STYLE

What if Benjy is your kid? No, you can't just walk out and pretend boisterous Benjy belongs to another parent. You are on the spot. What will you do?

Yes, being cool and a parent seems impossible. But when it comes to disciplining and raising your children, you can be a cool, wise parent. It depends on your disciplining response, and your response will depend on your style of parenting.

The *authoritarian* parent would say, "Benjy! Stop it, you are getting a spanking for this." The permissive parent would say, "Isn't that cute? Kids say the darndest things at this age. Little Benjy is getting so good with his colors."

I have actually read several articles and books on styles of parenting. I have come to a simple conclusion: You are either too rigid or too loose, and I'm not going to tell you which.

I get stressed out trying to analyze which style of parent I am. There are forms to complete. Checklists to consider. Self-tests to administer. It's a lot of work. In fact, just thinking about it makes me anxious.

What if I am the wrong style for my kid? I'm an out of style parent!

That's totally uncool!

I've got good news for you. Don't worry about what style of parent you are; just determine to parent with style. *Suave con estilo.*

BALANCED PARENTING

Parenting with style means balance. Sometimes you will need to be more of an authoritarian. Other times you will find a more permissive approach works.

Balanced parenting looks like this:

BALANCED PARENTING

The authoritative style offers balance between telling kids what to do and letting them do whatever they want. Our children may not need our continual instructions, but they do need our guidance. Balancing between being permissive and authoritarian isn't easy. It's like attempting to stand in the middle of a teeter-totter while it sways up and down. Your feet will tend to slide from one side to the other as you try to not fall off. And just when you think you've got it balanced, your kid puts her or his big toe on one end and your balance is lost.

Balance is a sign of maturity. It shows we aren't too extreme. Balance demonstrates we aren't reactionary. Some of the most neurotic parents I know are the ones who are trying to keep their kids from making mistakes. Some of the least effective are those who don't care.

Where can you find the right discipline style? The right stuff is found somewhere in the middle.

HELICOPTER PARENTS AND OSTRICH PARENTS

I've met two types of parents, both on either end of the parenting teeter-totter. The first are *Helicopter Parents*. They hover over their kids, swooping down just in time to deliver them from danger. Their goal is to deliver them from pain or discomfort. They are overly involved in their kids' lives. They make choices for their kids. This makes them good parents. At least, they think so.

Helicopter parents live vicariously through their kids. Their kids' failures are theirs (and a reflection of their parenting). They believe their kids' successes are largely due to their efforts.

The second type are *Ostrich Parents,* those with heads often buried in the sand. Ostrich parents have other things to occupy their interests. They reason that their child will "find his own way in his own time." Their motto is "Experience is a great teacher." Ostrich parents find the sand of their career, hobbies, or volunteer work far more interesting or rewarding than parenting. They are too busy to deal with some details of parenting.

Helicopter parents over-parent. Ostrich parents under-parent. Neither are relaxed parents.

Several years ago, I read the bestseller *In Search of Excellence,* by Tom Peters and Robert Waterman. One of their concepts was MBWA: Management By Wandering Around. It sounds goofy, and possibly too casual, but it has some great implications, especially for parenting.

Managers who are skilled in MBWA create an atmosphere for excellence. They wander around and foster a relaxed work environment. They trust their employees to do their job and believe that they want to achieve excellence. They aren't wandering around looking for mistakes, but for opportunities to motivate. They want to bring out the best of every employee.

PARENTING WITH STYLE

As I thought about MBWA, I thought it offered some ideas on how we can parent with style. How we can be parents and still be cool!

We need to relax. Don't take too much credit when our kids are good, and don't take too much blame when they aren't. In the in-flight magazine *Hemispheres,* family therapist and columnist John Rosemond wrote,

> The most effective parents, I realized, are those who are relaxed rather than constantly busy in their children's lives. Trusting that children want to become competent, they provide opportunities for growth, but allow their children a great deal of freedom

when it comes to choosing or rejecting these opportunities. Instead of taking credit when their children behave well and feeling guilty when their children behave poorly, they assign their children complete responsibility for their own behavior. They let their children make mistakes, realizing that the most valuable lessons in life are learned through trial and error.[1]

Many parents are well-intentioned, but lacking in style and technique.

They might be trying real hard, but they may be using the wrong tool. In fact, they may be trying too hard. Sometimes it's better to do less.

One day while working on my Triumph Spitfire, I dropped a socket deep into the engine cavity. I tried reaching it with the ratchet, but the tool was too fat. I reached with a screwdriver, but it wouldn't snag the socket. *I have to get this socket! I need it to do all this work!* I was getting mad.

Steve saw my frustration. He wiped his greasy forehead with his sleeve and asked, "Do you need some help?"

"Yeah, I dropped the 10 millimeter socket behind the manifold and I can't get it."

Steve pulled his red, cotton mechanic's rag from his pocket and wiped his hands. He reached for his Craftsman® twelve-drawer tool box and walked toward me. He had a smirk on his grimy face. Quickly, he slid open drawer seven and pulled out something that looked like a snake. Black at the head and red at the tail.

"Where did you drop it?"

"Right back there behind that flange on the manifold."

Steve deftly maneuvered the mechanical coral snake.

"Click."

"Got it!" Steve announced proudly.

"Wow, what is that magic tool?"

"It's a magnet, Einstein. It flexes. You can reach anything with this baby. You gotta have the right tool for the job."

Steve was only seventeen, but he was right. "You gotta have the right tool for the job." Whether it's auto mechanics, or parenting.

That's what this book is all about. Giving you tools so you can have the confidence that you will have the right parenting tool for the job. One of the critical tools is balance. Some parents have a tendency to relate to their child as "boss." They expect their child to quickly obey and never challenge. They often say, "Because I said so." When a parent loses his balance and becomes authoritarian we'll see:

- an attempt to control the child
- guilt used to manipulate
- an arrogant use of authority
- using arguments to force compliance
- anger towards, and possible verbal abuse of the child

The authoritarian parent may have the right goal: "Make my child do the right thing," but he may be using the wrong tool. The intentions are commendable; the approach isn't. This is where balance comes in. An authoritarian parent seeking balance might pause and ask:

- "Is my approach working?"
- "Is this really an issue of their behavior, or my expectations?"
- "If they only worked on one thing, what would it be?"
- "How is our relationship? What can I do to help it?"

Sometimes an authoritarian parent is so focused on getting his way that he "wins the battle and loses the war." He gains compliance but loses the relationship with his child. Balance for an authoritarian parent is taking time and effort to work on the relationship and evaluate expectations to see if they are realistic.

When a permissive parent loses balance we will see one or more of the following:

- the child's lack of respect for authority (hers and others')
- the child's tendency to continually push the limits
- manipulative whining or demands by the child

- reactions of outrage when the child is asked to do something
- parental feelings of guilt or shame

If you are a permissive parent seeking balance, ask yourself the following:

- "When do I find myself giving in to my child?"
- "Why do I give in to my child?"
- "What would it look like if my child were to demonstrate respect for my authority as a parent?"
- "What is one boundary I'd like to see recognized by my child (regardless of his/her negative reaction)?"

The permissive parent often gets caught up in the loop of wanting her child to like her. It's hard for her to say no. Balance, for her, will be to establish boundaries for her child and communicate them. Develop consequences for breaking them. Stick to them even if they complain.

Parents who rear their children with style act as Authoritative Parents. They know how to effectively use their authority as parents. They have confidence in their position. They know what they want from their children. The authoritative parent communicates his/her expectations to their children. They build in consequences for misbehavior. They aren't always on their kids to follow the rules. They know that kids will make mistakes. Sometimes they let them. They want them to learn from their choices. They want their kids to know that they are responsible for their choices.

The relaxed parent is the authoritative parent, one who balances rules with relationship.

Reflections

FOR THE RELAXED PARENT

1. Do you lean towards the Authoritarian Parent side, or towards the Permissive Parent side?
2. Would you classify yourself as a Helicopter Parent or an Ostrich Parent?
3. What healthy authority characteristics do you display in your parenting?
4. What is your greatest weakness in the exercise of your parental authority?

Skill Builder

BALANCE BUILDER

Think about the principle "Rules without relationship lead to rebellion."

What is one way you could enhance your relationship with your child this week?

When will you do it?

What is one rule that is really important to you? Have you told your child what that rule is, and why it is so important to you? How does not following this rule hurt your child? Does your child understand that this rule is for his/her protection and growth?

When will you tell him/her?

Make a four-week commitment to do something each week that reinforces your relationship with your child and reinforces this most important rule.

$\mathcal{P}$ARENTING $\mathcal{P}$RINCIPLE

The relaxed parent has realistic expectations—
of himself and of his children.

THREE

PARENTING
IN REALITY

$\mathcal{I}$n his delightful book called *Fatherhood*, actor/comedian Bill Cosby gives advice that is both wise and witty:

> No matter how much the pressure on your spinal cord builds up, never let these small people know that you have gone insane. There is an excellent reason for this:
> THEY WANT THE HOUSE.
> At the first sign that something is wrong with you, they will take you right to a home.
> When I reach sixty-five, I plan to keep a gun in my hand, for I know that the moment I spill something on my lap, they'll come to me and say, "We're sorry, Dad, but you can't control yourself and you've got to go."
> Whether or not I manage to avoid eviction, I hope that these young adversaries appreciate that my wife and I have tried not to make the mistakes that our parents made with us. For example, we have always been against calling the children idiots. This philosophy has been basic for my wife and me. And we proudly lived by it until the children came along.[1]

If you're like Bill Cosby, trying not to repeat the mistakes of your parents, then you probably remember the first time you spoke the words that you swore you would *never* say. You know what I'm talking about: Words Your Parents Used.

When did you first hear yourself say, "This is going to hurt me more than it's going to hurt you," or "I'm doing this for your own good"? These are scary moments when we repeat the script of our parents.

A True Confession

I swore I'd never say that sentence. It seemed so rote, so cliché. Every parent in my parents' generation must have said it. But I was going to stop it. Someone had to stop the growing brawl.

I was watching our two girls play at the neighborhood park. They had finished sliding and swinging and now proceeded to play in the sand. It started to get out of hand.

"I want my shovel back."

"No, you can't have it. Mine!"

"Oh yeah?" Brooke threw sand at Nicole.

"Ouch! You little brat!" Nicole threw a bigger handful of sand at Brooke.

"Missed me. Take this!" Brooke threw a bucketful of sand in Nicole's face.

Then it happened. I must have snapped. I said the forbidden words. Call me crazy. Call me a stressed-out parent. Call me my father's son.

"Stop it! *It's all fun and games until someone gets an eye poked out!*"

Whew! I feel better just admitting that. Confession is good for the soul. Now don't get too self-righteous. You say silly phrases like that, too! That's proof that you are a parent. I think I was a lot more articulate before I had kids. They have a way of bringing out the most inane comments in us.

Great Expectations, Fewer Resources

What is reality for a parent? What is reasonable to expect? First, let's recognize that being a parent is not getting easier. Being a parent in the 1990s means dealing with inflated expectations and diminishing resources. Let's consider first the fewer resources. We used to be able to count on our extended family nearby. Today, our children's aunts and uncles may visit once a year if we are lucky. Often they live out of state. Extended family members may be spread all over the country. Grandma probably isn't around to help with the kids.

What about our neighbors to help with our children? Years ago we could count on our neighbors, but we don't know them now. Whether it's our schedules, their schedules, or indifference, we don't seem to have the time to build friendships with those who live a few feet away. So they don't know us and can hardly help our children.

Parents used to depend on the resource of the stay-at-home mom. Those days are gone. In some areas, 80 percent of the mothers work outside the home. They have to, just to make ends meet. Many of them are single mothers. They want to do a good job being a mom. They have high aspirations. They too are facing *inflated expectations and diminishing resources*.

Parenting in the 1990s is made tougher by the expectations we parents bring to our roles. Parenting *in reality* begins with our having an accurate picture of what makes a good parent.

Most parents picture the ideal American father as "one who works hard, is a good provider and comes home and wrestles with the kids, or plays ball with them."[2] The ideal mother, to most women, keeps the children happy and helps them avoid pain and hardship. But our own images of what makes a good father or a good mother are based on what culture tells us at the moment, or comparing our parenting with that of someone else.

Marty's Story

Clinical psychologists Faber and Mazlish illustrate faulty parenting expectations with Marty's story. This father, home from the hospital after a heart attack, felt frustrated that he couldn't play immediately with his boys.

One day he heard one of his sons tell the other, "Daddy isn't the same. He never boxes with us anymore or carries us up to bed. He won't even play baseball with us!"

The words depressed Marty. His wife, Evelyn, later told a parents' support group she attended, "He feels he isn't being a real father to his boys anymore."

Leading Evelyn's group was Haim Ginott, noted psychologist and lecturer. He listened sympathetically. The following exchange illustrates both Marty's and Evelyn's faulty expectations about being parents. Dr. Ginott spoke first.

"Evelyn, being a father has nothing to do with boxing or baseball. I know the picture of Dad out there in the park, pitching and catching with his sons, is very attractive. But baseball can be taught by anyone. A father's job is to help his son feel good about himself."

"Feel good about himself?" Evelyn echoed anxiously.

Dr. Ginott elaborated. "A father's most important job is to help his children like themselves—to communicate to them that they're fine human beings, worthy of respect, a pleasure to be with, people whose feelings and ideas have value.

"The boys are upset about the new restrictions on them. Having to be quiet. Not having friends over. They are not happy about it."

Dr. Ginott spoke with a trace of impatience in his voice. "Evelyn, is it a parent's function to keep his children happy all the time?"

"Not exactly," Evelyn protested, "but no mother wants to see her children looking sad or in tears."

"For me," Dr. Ginott answered, "a child's laughter and his tears have equal importance. I would not want to take away from him disappointment, sorrow, grief. Emotions ennoble character. The deeper we feel, the more human we become."

Silence.

"I ought to know better by now! You've said a hundred times that our job isn't to make our children happy, but to help them become more human. How often do I have to hear that thought before it becomes a part of me?" asked Evelyn.

Dr. Ginott made a gesture of resignation. "How many times do we have to tune a violin before it stays tuned?"

Evelyn had come to the meeting with two preconceived notions of what a parent should be—the father who plays ball with his sons, the mother dedicated to her children's happiness. Neither of these notions had been helpful to her or her family. And she would leave today with two very different interpretations of the parents' role, hopefully interpretations that would serve everyone better.[3]

We have expectations in our minds about the good parent. When we come close to meeting those expectations, we feel content and competent. When we don't, we feel guilty or anxious. Not living up to our expectations makes us feel like losers.

Parent Support Groups: Reality-Check Time

Evelyn benefited from her parents' support group. In this group she received input, affirmation, and support. She wasn't alone in her parenting struggles. In this group she also discovered parenting in reality.

I heartily commend parent support groups to help moms and dads discover reality in their parenting. Committed to truth, parent groups are great places to get a "reality check." As parents, we all live in a certain degree of denial, often about our kids' weaknesses. Such denial helps us to cope. But sometimes we need to break through the denial and have an accurate assessment of what's going on in our family. It's hard to do that alone.

I remember the endorsements for such support groups at the end of a ten-week scheduled parents' group a few years ago. It sounded like a testimonial meeting for Alcoholics Anonymous; each of us seemed to have found a distortion that our discussion had pointed out or a session topic had exposed. We were better parents for it.

We had met for nine Wednesday nights in a large home in Westlake Village, California. The topic of our meetings was "Empowering Tools for Parents." More than a dozen parents attended. Our group included a few single parents. Like most support groups, we agreed to a set number of weeks and had a facilitator to lead them. Usually, parents groups make a three-to-six month commitment to attend. Sometimes it's helpful to share the facilitating of the discussion. That way no one is perceived as the expert.

But in this situation, I was the primary facitator. As the group leader, I asked the parents at our tenth and final meeting to describe the impact of our times together.

Here are some of their responses:

"I think I have shifted my thoughts on communication," said Cindy. "I used to try and communicate with my teen like I would with an adult. I thought a good parent had these intense and satisfying discussions with her daughter. Now I understand that teenagers don't communicate the same way adults do. I don't feel the pressure to be the effective communicator. I just listen and talk."

"What really got me was the stuff on anger," admitted Ed. "I struggle with my temper. Just ask Dolores here. Anyway, I used to think that a good parent never yelled; he kept his anger to himself. Now I'm realizing that I need to express my anger. Not swear at the kid, but let him know I'm angry. I tried it the other day. Instead of steaming inside, I said, 'Luis, I am really angry with you for trashing the garage.'

"And you know what he said? 'Sorry, Dad, I'll clean it up right now.'"

Ed smiled. He had shifted from the bottle-your-anger dad to the express-your-anger-but-not-destructively dad. It felt liberating.

Communication and honest emotions were two major topics we had discussed, so I was not surprised at their impact on Cindy and Ed. Most parents have expectations, many unrealistic, about how they should express themselves to their children. They involve issues of openness and relationship that we will discuss in upcoming chapters.

"Feelings have always been a tough one for me," Bruce said. "As a police officer I've been trained to be objective. To be in control emotionally. I brought this approach home with me. It worked better in law enforcement than at home. My paradigm shift occurred when I discovered that feelings aren't right or wrong—they just are. What's important is how we deal with them. It's freed me up from a lot of shame. I now see my feelings as a potential asset to parenting, not a liability."

"I think for me, I learned to shift from the do-it-all mom," said Elaine. "I used to be willing to do anything for my kids. I tried to find solutions to all their problems. I tried to keep them from any discomfort. Now I realize that sometimes parents *help most by not helping*. My reality check came when I realized I was doing too much. I need to let them experience some failure and pain. That helps them learn responsibility."

"My kids' behavior was destroying me," declared Charlene. "I came to this group looking for answers, looking for support— actually, looking for a miracle. As a single mom, I really needed a reality check. Was it me or my kids? What has helped me in this group has been the discussions on discipline versus punishment. I used to use more of a punishment approach. You know, a lot of yelling and threats. Now, I am more emotionally detached and simply review the consequences. I used to think parents had to control their kids; now I see it has more to do with teaching and relationship."

Those were five discoveries made by various members of the group. But there were four others, dealing with negative emotions, consequences, avoiding shame, and using healing words. Each suggests a practical principle of parenting. Let's look at what the other four group members saw.

"'Words that heal.' That's what got to me," said Butch. "I used to think that it didn't matter what I said to my kids as long as I loved them. But that stuff on 'words that hurt' versus 'words that heal' really nailed me. Now I realize the incredible power of words to shape our kids' feelings about themselves, and even their behavior. I discovered a very powerful tool for motivation and affirmation. Now, my kids don't have to read my mind to know how I feel about them. I tell them."

Janice talked about her two daughters, only thirteen months apart. The two were in the throes of sibling rivalry. "It got so bad, I wasn't sure they'd live to be in junior high. I thought they might kill each other!" Janice told us.

"I didn't know what to do with these strong, negative emotions," Janice continued. "I used to say, 'You really don't *hate* your sister. Deep down you really love her.'"

Now Janice has begun trying to identify with the particular daughter's emotion, not just correct it. "When we acknowledge our child's emotion it actually gives her strength to deal with it," Janice recognized. "I wasn't comfortable with their anger. Now I realize I'm not responsible for it."

"Consequences and decision-making were the topics that caused me the greatest need for adjustment in my perspective," Gordon said. "You'd think that as an engineer, I'd know how important the law of cause and effect is. But I was parenting as if it didn't apply to our family. I used to think that a good parent makes decisions that are best for his children. I have come to understand that a good parent *prepares* his children to make good decisions. But he gives them freedom to make them on their own. That way they learn. We need to give them life-skills. They won't always have us with them."

Maria had one final personal discovery to share with the group. She began by telling us about her own family. "I came from a very strict, religious home. My parents believed in the philosophy that if you tell a child what is wrong with her, she'll improve. They thought if they called me stupid, I'd become smart. If they called me a liar, I'd be honest. They even called me 'slut,' hoping I'd stay a virgin. I never realized how my parents' perception of me shaped my self-image." She paused.

"Through this group I learned that a good parent doesn't shame children into anything. But a good parent treats her children with dignity and respect. Helping them picture all that they can be. A good parent sees potential in her children that the child may not be able to see in herself."

NINE PRINCIPLES FOR PARENTING IN REALITY

Those parents had recited nine principles they had discovered during our ten weeks of presentation and dialogue. They are not all the truths of parenting, but they contain many solid nuggets. Let me summarize them, for they help all of us to rear our children in reality:

1. Children don't communicate the same way adults do. Trying to communicate like an adult only leads to frustration. Focus on listening and tuning into the emotions, rather than the actual words.

2. Parenting can be extremely frustrating. If you are angry, say so. But do it in such a way that it doesn't insult or blame.

3. Trying to "do it all" is a guaranteed path to burnout. Sometimes we help our kids most by not helping.

4. Feelings aren't good or bad; they just are.

5. Punishment as a means of correction isn't enough. We need to teach our children appropriate behavior through discipline.

6. Words have tremendous power to heal, affirm, and guide our children.

7. When we acknowledge our child's strong negative emotions instead of trying to change them, we communicate acceptance at a time when our child needs it the most.

8. We help our child by preparing him/her to make good decisions. One way we do this is teaching by using consequences.

9. We communicate dignity and respect to our child. We avoid shaming her/him.

Parenting isn't an exact science. It's more of an art. But when we have principles that have been forged through experience, we have the tools to shape our art form. There are no guarantees in parenting. No fool-proof formulas. Our kids have a way of tampering with our formulas anyway. What worked for the first kid won't work for the second. All the more reason why we should stay current with our parenting.

Being realistic is the first step to being effective. Trying to be the perfect parent is the fast lane to insanity. When it comes to parenting, reality is a good place to start.

Reflections

FOR THE RELAXED PARENT

1. Did you ever say something to your child that you intended to never say?
2. How do you know if you are "parenting in reality"?
3. Does it seem to you that we are parenting in a culture with inflated expectations and diminished resources?
4. Describe the Ideal Dad and the Ideal Mom.
5. What do you think about Ginott's comment, "It is the father's job to help his son feel good about himself"?
6. How did Evelyn benefit from her parents' group?
7. Which person in the parents' group do you most closely identify with?
8. Which of the "Nine Principles for Parenting in Reality" would you like to implement?

EDUCATIONAL TV

Review the "Nine Principles for Parenting in Reality." Choose three that you'd like to discuss as a family. Many of these apply to children as much as to us parents. For example, "Feelings aren't good or bad; they just are," is a reality our children need to think about as much as we do.

Record the three selected principles on a piece of poster paper in large letters and display them above the television set. Choose a TV show that features a family. Provide everyone with pencil and paper. Watch the show together and see how many times the characters follow or ignore these three principles. For instance, one of your principles could be:

2. "Parenting can be extremely frustrating. If you are angry, say so. But do it in such a way that it doesn't insult or blame."

Some shows demonstrate people handling anger in a healthy way; most don't. See if your children notice this. Afterward, serve up some ice cream and discuss what you observed. Compare your findings.

*P*ARENTING
*P*RINCIPLE

*The relaxed parent understands
the trends affecting children in order
to understand his own children.*

FOUR

HURRIED, HASSLED, AND HUSHED

*W*hen I was thirteen I didn't realize that I was contributing to a social phenomenon. I just wanted some laughs. How was I to know that my friends and I were ushering in a revolution of free expression? No, we weren't ready to march against the Vietnam War nor take some White Album Beatles–induced trip down Penny Lane. We just wanted to enjoy the literary choice of young adolescent males. If you were male and had this magazine of sophistication, you had class. (You also had friends, because they would read over your shoulder.) Of course, I am referring to that erudite journal of humor, *Mad* magazine.

Don't tell my mom, but I had tons of them. She didn't like *Mad*, though at the time I wasn't sure why. We guys loved to read *Mad*. We would save up our paper route money and head off to the convenience store to buy the latest edition. Since our parents didn't like us reading what they called "sarcastic pulp," we had to find a place to stash our collection. The summer I turned thirteen we built a tree house. It served three purposes: (1) to get away from our parents, (2) to get away from our little brothers, and (3) to indulge in a bash of *Mad*.

We would spend hours in our tree house. Laughing and learning. We began to look at our world differently. *Mad* shaped our world. We were not alone; across the country, millions of teens chuckled and made some shifts in their thinking.

Al Feldstein, editor-in-chief of *Mad* for over twenty-five years, once described the magazine's philosophy. (Yes, *Mad* magazine has a philosophy.)

> What we did was to take the absurdities of the adult world and show kids that adults are not omnipotent. That their parents were being two-faced in their standards—telling kids to be honest, not to lie, and yet themselves cheating on their income tax. We showed kids that the world out there is unfair, that a lot of people out there are lying to them, cheating them. We told them there's a lot of garbage in the world and you've got to beware of it. Everything you read in the papers is not necessarily true. What you see on television is mostly lies. You're going to have to learn to think for yourself.[1]

Mad magazine ushered kids from innocence to reality. The notion that childhood was a protected time was not acknowledged by this popular magazine. If it was fair for adults, it was fair for kids.

Growing up, I was taught to trust people. To respect them and their views. In the tree house with my copy of *Mad*, I learned to distrust people. To make fun of their views.

The parodies in the monthly became increasingly more adult. Sexuality, adultery, homosexuality, drug and alcohol abuse, divorce, violence, and rape. Each topic was open for satire.

Comparing an issue of *Mad* of the 1980s with one from the 1950s provides an almost shocking view of the change that childhood had undergone in those years. The magazine of December 1980, for example, features a parody of the movie *Little Darlings*, a film about two thirteen-year-old girls at summer camp who have a race to see which of them can lose her virginity first. The version includes an outdoor salesman hawking a new kind of children's wares: "Get your training diaphragms here!" he cries. "She's starting foreplay now."[2]

Now I see why my mom didn't want me to be exposed to this stuff.

Mad magazine didn't cause social decline in America; it reflected it. There is a lot of garbage in the world, but kids used to be protected from it. Now they see it live as the "latest news bulletin with a developing story."

My research has led me to note some trends in childhood. Through the reading of popular and professional works, along with my own work with youth, I have discovered ten trends. They indicate what is happening to large numbers of children. As a parent, you can learn a lot by looking at the "herd" with which your child or adolescent roams. You can understand your own child better by seeing what most children face. Here's what it's like growing up in America.

TEN TRENDS IN CHILDHOOD

1. Less Supervision

When I went to our tree house, Mom knew where I was. She stayed at home with four kids. When I went to the tree house she probably enjoyed the break from me, too! If I needed her, like the time I fell out of the tree house, all I had to do was send for her. She was at home. She was available. I could count on it.

Mom also seemed to have a sixth sense about what I was up to. Like that time I had a bunch of cherry bombs and was planning to put them down the toilets at school. Somehow she found out and confiscated them. How did she know? Does the FBI report to Mom?

Anyway, mothers are far less likely to be at home during weekday working hours in the 1990s. In fact, a majority of women with children are working mothers, and in homes throughout America's suburbs, so-called "latch-key children" have their own house keys and come home with neither mother nor father waiting for them. They are unsupervised or else the child-watcher is the friendly baby-sitter. Friendly, but usually not related and certainly less able to give the love a parent can when comfort is needed.

Marie Winn, author of the best-selling book *Children Without Childhood*, described the implications of children being home with little supervision.

Children are likely to receive less care and supervision than they enjoyed with a stay-at-home mother, wretched and unhappy though she may have been. Such children are more likely, in today's social and cultural environment, to infiltrate adult life and find themselves partaking of adult experiences that they are developmentally unprepared to deal with. While they may survive, they are less likely than their more protected counterparts to attain their optimal emotional growth and to reach maturity unscathed.[3]

Less supervision leads to more independence. Children are left alone at an earlier age. They are expected to become independent and often are hurried to achieve separation from parents. They are being rushed towards independence.

2. Too Many Choices

I grew up without a TV. We had three choices: read, play, or listen to the stereo. This last one really wasn't much of a choice. The only music my parents had was classical. When I was eleven we finally got a television set. A used console, black and white, of course. We watched "Lassie," "Ted Mack's Amateur Hour," "Ed Sullivan," and Saturday morning cartoons. We had three networks to choose from, and the reception was fuzzy.

Kids today have over 140 cable choices on their 27-inch color TV with stereo sound. And that's the one in their bedroom. If you really want a good picture, go downstairs to the family's home theater: big screen with high-tech Dolby noise reduction and four-channel sound. The technology rivals the best of the movie theaters from our childhood.

Now it takes a TV viewing guide the size of a Milwaukee phone book just to select what show we'll watch. Too many choices. It's enough to stress you out.

And it does.

Kids are being faced with other choices as well, choices and situations that used to be restricted to adults. They range from teenage pregnancy to neighborhood crime. Douglas Nelson, executive director of the Casey Foundation, (which studies family issues), says these situations leave children unprepared for parenthood.

Worsening high school graduation rates, increasing births to single teenagers and widening exposure to community violence and crime guarantee that a large number of our young adults will enter parenthood unprepared to raise their own children.[4]

Kids used to worry about getting teased on the school bus. Now they worry about getting shot or stabbed. Seemingly to compensate for the pressures of these adult-like situations, our children have been given more freedom to choose. But they are no better prepared to make the decisions than you or I were as children. Most don't have the critical decision-making skills to choose wisely. David Elkind, psychology professor at Tufts University, explains our children's dilemma:

> Young people today, for example, are freer than ever before to engage in sexual activity, to abuse drugs, and to flout adult authority. At the same time, they are less prepared than ever before to manage these new freedoms.[5]

3. A Rush to Adulthood

With Dad and Mom rushing off to work, child care becomes a burden. Parents come home tired from the job, full of tension from the rush-hour drive, and perhaps irritated with a coworker. In this environment we can think our children are a nuisance at times. In fact, we can forget our children are just that—children. Instead of sheltering them and bestowing our love, we can treat our kids like another task. We want them to grow up in a hurry, and we don't protect them from the worries of the adult world.

In doing that, we are promoting the disappearance of childhood, according to sociologist and commentator Neil Postman. In his pioneering book entitled *The Disappearance of Childhood,* Postman issued a warning:

> As parents of both sexes make their way in the world, children become something of a burden, and increasingly, it is deemed best that their childhood end as early as possible. . . . Unless there occurs a 180 degree turn in social trends, the American family will not

stand in strong opposition to the contraction and then dissolution of childhood.[6]

I believe that Postman is warning us of the trend to treat kids like adults, to minimize the differences between the two. When we reduce the natural boundary that separates childhood from adulthood, we rush our kids into situations they are not equipped to handle. They are no longer protected, but hurried. And hurried children, notes Elkind, "are stressed by the fear of failure—of not achieving fast enough or high enough. Hurried children are forced to take on the physical, psychological, and social trappings of adulthood before they are prepared to deal with them."[7]

4. Loss of Innocence

All this adult-like behavior and exposure leads to a loss of childlike innocence. It reminds me of a story my friend told me.

"I was complaining to my wife about the wild parties in our apartment complex. I told her, 'Hey, look at this! They left beer cans and trash all over. I even found a condom on the patio!' My eight-year-old son overheard me talk, and before my wife could answer, he asked a question.

"'Dad. What's a patio?'"

His child is like most children. Our kids these days are exposed to things we didn't know about until college (and then we weren't quite sure).

A good example of this ebbing of innocence can be seen by popular children's literature. One of the best-selling series is R. L. Stine's "Fear Street." The books feature murder, gore, stalkers, and ghosts. It's Stephen King for kids. Things have come a long way since Nancy Drew Mysteries or the Hardy Boys.

And then we have the Judy Blume genre. This group of writers pens short novels for children ages eight to sixteen, a segment referred to by some as the "young adult" market. Our third-graders read about characters that are presented as miniature adults. The characters may be twelve, but they are facing adult-like situations. Which parent should I live with after divorce? What am I going to do about this jerk my mom married that I have to call "dad"? Such "reality-based" writing is forcing children to deal with their own situations of living in a single-parent household, for instance, or to deal with the stressful situations of their friends.

Even movie studios have gotten in on the act. Kids used to build clubhouses and go on adventures with their pets. Now they "borrow" Dad's credit card, charge up enough debt to burden a third world country, and go on adventures to New York where they pummel bad guys. *Home Alone* is a long leap from *Lassie Come Home*.

5. More Single Parents

Of all the trends creating stress on childhood, none has had greater ramifications than children growing up in one-parent families. Divorce means the children in the household are reared by a mother or a father, but not both. Winn is accurate when she writes: "The disappearance of marriage as a dependable, permanent structure within which children can live out their childhood is surely the most consequential change that has occurred in the last two decades."[8]

Divorce has dramatically altered the scene of the American home. Not only does it create two single parents, but it also introduces a glut of questions and situations that are new to the kids. Perhaps most significant, children of divorce have their parents' fallibility thrust upon them long before they reach the developmental point of separation and independence:

> Children of divorce are made to understand in specific detail that their parents are often as helpless and confused as they themselves are. In the past, this was a discovery that children made slowly and painfully during the course of their adolescence; when they finally came to grips with the realization that their parents were just normal, fallible human beings, they were often ready to take the last step towards separating emotionally from their parents and starting an independent life. They were on the verge of adulthood.[9]

In addition, the child begins to consider the question "whether consciously articulated or not: *Who will take care of me if my parents can't even take care of themselves?*"[10]

6. No More Heroes

Kids used to have heroes who could be role models. Now they have celebrities. The well-known are often notorious. Michael Jackson becomes known for suspected child molestation; Madonna is notable for a book of provocative adult poses. The heroes are seldom healthy role models. Probably the closest thing to a hero would be nonhuman: Ninja Turtles; or semi-human: Mighty Morphin Power Rangers.

Even sports heroes are now suspect. From Magic Johnson's admission of having HIV to Dennis Rodman's sulking, referee-baiting, and multicolored hairdos, several sports stars are less than heroic. They have admitted or been accused of drug addictions, sexual promiscuity, gambling, wife abuse, and whining about money. It's enough to make you want to skip the game and stay home and watch *A League of Their Own* on video.

Wasn't it Charles Barkley who said, "I'm no role model?" With his fighting, complaining, and yelling at referees, I have to agree.

Kids have a hard time looking up to heroes. But then, they have a hard time looking up to adults. In *Teenage Wasteland*, Donna Gaines noted that children have little respect for adults, who have portrayed kids in movies and television as "troubled and troublesome reminders of social decay." She concluded,

> Dramatized in a rhetoric of despair, each new youth atrocity was sensationalized. When American youth were not viewed as our victims, we were viewed as theirs. Our social contract with our youth has become null and void. *Adults have lost their legitimacy as trustworthy authority figures.*[11]

If adults can't be trusted, who do children look to for examples? They look to each other. Kids set the standards for kids. They try to show each other the way.

Children in our country are desperately in need of guides—people who know the path and are willing to show the way.

7. Blurring of Roles and Boundaries

Not too long ago, kids were kids and adults were adults. Now it's kind of blurry. Adults acting like kids. Kids pretending they are adults. It's confusing.

We used to say, "Not in front of the children." Childhood was seen as a time of innocence and protection; certain topics were not discussed in front of children. Now, in the Information Age, all subjects are easy-access to minors.

The concept of childhood depends on a commitment to keep information from children, to recognize that certain information is age-sensitive. Adults used to keep secrets; there are no more secrets. In fact, we feel funny keeping things from our kids. "They have a right to know." Or do they?

Modern communication contributes greatly to the blurring of the lines between childhood and adulthood. Two technologies largely responsible for pulling down boundaries and making children grow up prematurely are computer modems and television sets.

My daughter Nicole went to a friend's house, and they spent hours communicating online to teenage boys throughout the country. The boys flirted with them and asked what they looked like. Some of the guys made suggestive comments. Nicole told me she typed, "You are rude and a loser. Get lost!" and flushed him out of the "room."

It's the 1990s and children are swapping information online. They are even being sexually harassed via modem.

Parents cannot easily manage information that is not delivered sequentially—based on children's developmental stages—and that's the problem with the computer Internet and TV shows.

Yet the need for us parents to monitor our children's information flow still exists. Remember when our sons and daughters were small? We put dangerous or breakable items on the top shelf, out of reach. We did this for their welfare; we even locked the lower cabinets with child-safety locks. Our kids were restricted from things that might hurt them. It might be old-fashioned and discriminatory, but we loved our daughters enough to keep certain things from them. Parents need to restore the "top shelf." There are certain things that younger children shouldn't be exposed to until they are older.

The top shelf is being replaced by the computers and TVs. Both are very democratic—everyone is considered equal. Everyone is a consumer. Consider television. Because it doesn't discriminate what it shows, it effectively destroys any hierarchy of information. Postman lists three ways that TV has removed the boundaries between children and adults.

- TV is user-friendly. Anyone can operate a TV. A viewer doesn't require instruction to be entertained or informed by TV.
- TV doesn't demand much. No behavior or deep thought is required in this passive medium.
- TV doesn't segregate its audience. It is the total disclosure medium. (If you have any doubts, look at the topics on daily talk shows.)[12]

On the TV screen everyone is equal. In fact, the kids seem to be smarter and more in charge than the adults. Most sitcoms show inept parents and cool, competent kids.

In addition, living arrangements at home may give the child early exposure to adult experiences. For instance, in a single parent household, what should a seven-year-old think of mom's boyfriend sleeping over? In a two-parent, two-income home, how is a twelve-year-old girl supposed to deal with her first period when she is home alone one afternoon?

Children of divorce also face an early introduction into the world of the adult. Winn reports that "Researchers have discovered that family breakup increases a child's vulnerability to the stresses of modern life." She adds, "Statistically, children of divorce are more likely to become involved with alcohol and drugs, to commit suicide, to get in trouble with the law, to fail in school."[13] Talk about children having to grow up fast. This hardly sounds like the *Brady Bunch*.

8. The End of Play

Children often have busy schedules, so busy that their play is scheduled, structured, and not always relaxing. Hurried kids work much more than they play. After seven hours in school, they may rush off to a soccer practice, then home for a quick dinner, followed by piano practice and homework. For many, the weekends are even busier. They range from Little League coaches and tutors to treachers giving private music lessons, dance instruction, martial arts instructions, and for us near Hollywood, acting lessons. Then we have in-home child-care providers, maids, the pool man, the car wash guy, and the youth director or Sunday school teacher at church.

All these add up to representatives for us. They are substitutes for what parents used to do. We want our kids to have it all and do it all, but we are too busy to do it all with them. So we arrange subs. By scheduling all of their free time we also stifle our children's creativity. Such scheduling also limits our children's experiences with us.

When do children have time to imagine? When is there time to make-believe? Some of the saddest kids I know are the most hurried. They are continually rushed off to "their" activities, rather than be home with their family to play and imagine. Given the chance, many of them would like to stay home and play.

Imaginary play is stress-reducing for kids. Nothing is expected of them. They don't have to perform. No one is watching, or demanding. They can be anyone they want. They can be anywhere they want. Then, in the middle of it, they can stop, switch, and be someone else, somewhere else. It's really fun. That's why it's called play. It's rare.

For those who have the time, the games are passive and not creative: Playing computer games or watching video movies is a common pastime. In fact, some children fill their day staring at the TV, switching from video games, to video movies, to TV and back. Surrogates are nice in helping busy parents, but imagination and relaxation require simple schedules and parents being around to stimulate their kids' minds. (We don't even need to participate in their games to stimulate them. We only need to know their needs and give suggestions.)

9. Critical Decisions Too Early

Children are often introduced to situations that demand their assessment. They are forced to make a critical decision before they have the necessary skills. We used to take comfort that our kids would not be damaged by information over their heads because *they will only absorb as much as they are ready for.*

Recently, the popular TV show "Cybill" depicted the teenage daughter pretending she was thinking of becoming a lesbian. Her aim was to confuse her mother, Cybill, and sneak out of the house to rendezvous with her boyfriend. Teenagers watching this "family" show were sure to get a mixed message on the important subject of sexual orientation. At a time when teenage children need clarity and assurance, they are offered confusion. The story line got laughs, but it forced teenage viewers to make a premature assessment. Children should be able to watch television without wondering, *Am I gay?*

Children absorb whatever they are exposed to. They may not fully understand, but they will process it the best they can, and it will have an impact. It won't go over their heads if they aren't ready for it. It will go *into* their heads—ready or not.

10. Receiving Parents' Money Instead of Time

With Mom and Dad both at work, time has become a precious commodity. Children often receive their parents' love in the form of tokens and clothing, but they prefer to receive their parents' time. Many parents sacrifice *their* pleasures trying to help their children with needs, though sometimes they actually are indulging their children's wants. When was the last time *you* had $140 Air Jordan shoes?

If you are a single parent, time is like gold. Many parents have to work harder just to make ends meet. Yet we parents must be careful that, in our long hours, we don't spend money on our children without spending time on them. One does not replace the other.

Our kids are trained by peers and TV to become consumers. Some really believe "it's the shoes." There's an expectation for acquiring certain key items. In some cities it might be shoes; in others, it might be clothes. In our local mall, the hip store this year sells pagers. Many teenagers feel they "need" a pager.

Our children have high expectations for "stuff." As busy parents, we often give in. Guilt drives us to indulge our kids. We feel bad about all the time we spend at work, so we try to replace ourselves with stuff. We want to teach our kids that "people are more important than things," but if we can't be around, we pay them off with things.

THE OUTCOME: STRESS

Because of these ten trends in childhood, our children face major stresses growing up. By the time they reach adolescence, our children are going to be hurried, hassled, and hushed. They'll be hushed because adults have failed to take them seriously. They'll be hushed because adults haven't taken time to listen. They'll be hushed because they won't be focusing on talking, but on coping. Elkind concludes,

> Teenagers today are under more psychological stress than ever before. To make matters worse, a large proportion of today's teenagers have one or another variety of patchwork self, which renders them vulnerable to stress. This lethal combination of increased stress and increased numbers of teenagers who are vulnerable to stress has produced the alarming increase in destructive stress reactions that characterizes the contemporary generation of teenagers.[14]

Kids these days are hurried, hassled, and hushed. As a result, they are also hostile. We see it in the news and in our neighborhoods: Gangs. Violence. Anger. Blame. Vengeance. Many of these teens are ticked off, and they aren't going to take it anymore.

Hostility is increasing. No wonder the media have labeled them "Children of Rage."

But that's not all bad.

When we, as an American people, get angry enough, we do something.

It's in our genes. It's part of our heritage. It's what July 4th is all about. I believe adults, and especially parents, want the children of this country to grow up loved and to develop into responsible and secure adults. Looking at these trends you may see issues involving your own children with which you want to deal.

In spite of these trends, I'm optimistic about this generation. The challenge is to find a way to acknowledge the hostility and direct the energy into something productive. For many of us, being aware of these trends is a start.

I believe that opportunity often comes disguised as opposition. With these difficult social trends we may be facing the most difficult decade to be a parent. We also may be facing the most important decade to be a parent.

Reflections

FOR THE RELAXED PARENT

1. When you were thirteen, where did you go to hang out with your friends? Did you have a tree house?
2. Do you think our culture seeks to end childhood as early as possible?
3. What parameters have you set in your family regarding TV viewing?
4. Do you think the borders between childhood and adulthood have eroded? Give examples for your position.
5. If kids are hurried, hassled, and hushed, they become hostile. Have you noticed an increase of hostility among youth in your community?
6. Do you agree with the author's assessment that these ten trends present an opportunity?

Skill Builder

MEDIA GLANCE

Choose a form of popular media: TV, music videos, movies, or magazines. Make a list of these ten trends in childhood. See how many are reflected in the medium you choose. Place a check by each trend every time there is a reference to it.

Compare and discuss your findings with your spouse or another parent.

$\mathcal{P}$ARENTING $\mathcal{P}$RINCIPLE

*The relaxed parent prepares
his children for life by treating them
as family members, not guests.*

FIVE

PRINCES AND PRINCESSES

Yeah, I work long hours, sometimes fourteen-hour days. But it's worth it. If it's busy, I make a lot of tips," explained Jose.

"Do you make more driving shuttle to the airport or around town?" I asked.

"The airport is much better. Much quicker. Sometimes I'll make twenty trips to LAX [Los Angeles International Airport] in one day. I've gone home on those days with two hundred dollars in tips. I like always having cash."

"I bet."

"You know what I do with the tips?"

"What?"

"Every day, I stop at the store and buy my kids something. A toy, some candy, a doll, some music—something they want."

"Jose, you mean you bring them little gifts like a squirt gun or gum, right?"

"No sir. I buy them nice presents. You know, from Toys R Us."

"Every day?"

"Yes sir, every day."

"How old are your kids?"

"Annabela is eight and Ricardo is ten. We just bought new furniture for Ricky. He has a whole new bedroom set. Matching. Looks good. Even the TV and desk match."

Jose smiled with pride as he drove me to the Burbank airport. I was astounded. Jose had been in the United States less than ten years. He had worked hard, saved his money, and bought a van with the airport shuttle company.

I was happy to see that Jose had done so well. As a citizen, he had effectively pursued life, liberty, and happiness. But as an American, he picked up a bad habit—spoiling his kids. I wondered if Annabela and Ricardo would have the same drive and perseverance as their dad. Would they have the character that he had? Or would they be like so many other American kids— spoiled rotten?

It doesn't take one long in our country to observe that many of our kids perceive themselves to be princes and princesses. They have high expectations. They have a taste for perfection. They have a distaste for discomfort. And they don't want to wait. Everything must be fun, and they must have it now.

BEING ABLE TO SAY NO TO OUR CHILDREN

As parents, we often cater to our children's every whim. We give so much of ourselves, but we receive so little in return. So many of us are like Jose, working hard, long hours to provide our kids with the best. But we have no guarantee that they will appreciate it. Though not a cultural theorist, Fred Gosman is a father who in his book *Spoiled Rotten* expresses what many parents have been feeling privately:

> We parents often try to give our children just about everything *we* can dream of. In doing so, we destroy the thrill and excitement that result only when treats are received *rarely*. Our children become jaded and unappreciative of all that they have, and they subsequently *expect* to get all that they want.[1]

Just because we can afford to buy something for our kids doesn't mean we should. They need to see us use restraint. They need to hear "No." They need to see us wait. Always delivering the goods robs our kids of the joy of anticipation. It replaces wonder with an ugly sense of entitlement. Many of our kids are becoming princes and princesses because they have seen it all and done it all. "Been there. Done that!" is the echo of our times. Our children become jaded because there are no more surprises. Life begins to feel like a rerun.

We rob our kids' dreams when we fulfill all their wishes. We take away that innocent, childlike anticipation.

THE JOY OF WAITING

One of my most memorable childhood memories was Christmas. We began the ritual by selecting and cutting down a tree. Boxes appeared, filled with decorations. We spent an evening trimming our tree. It was a lovely torture: The tinsel, ornaments, and lights would tease, "twenty-one days to Christmas." Twenty-one days is a long time for a child to wait.

The anticipation built in other ways. Packages from relatives began arriving in the mail. People stopped by to offer baked goods and candy. Colorful, interesting presents surrounded the tree, and the different shapes seemed to beckon that I touch them, lift them, shake them. My excitement was increasing. Wonder filled the air. *Would I get a slot-car race set? Could that big red box be it? Maybe I'll get a chemistry set—I could make stink bombs!*

Christmas wouldn't be Christmas if we removed the surprise. If we eliminated the wonder. If we hurried the process. The joy was in the wait. The excitement was in the anticipation. Maybe Christmas is supposed to be that way. After all, that first Christmas involved waiting. Mary and Joseph were full of anticipation. The Christmas story itself is full of surprise and wonder.

Christmas is special because of the wonder. We deprive our children of the joy of wonder when we deliver on demand. Or worse yet, deliver on whim. What's the solution? Make them wait. Let them wonder. That means telling them no. It seems cruel at first, but the thrill of anticipation your child feels in waiting is worth it.

Let's go back to my family Christmas. The scene in our Colorado home would have been ruined if my parents had placed *unwrapped* presents under the tree on December 1 and announced, "Here are the gifts you ordered. Everything just like you wrote on your Christmas Demand List. You can begin playing with them. Have a nice day."

The delight in Christmas is in the wishing. It's in the wonder.

In their loss of innocence our kids have lost their wonder. They have become so "bottom-line." "I want this, and I want it now," they tell us. Part of the problem is that they are a generation raised on selection. They have been trained by TV and their friends to be consumers who want to have and to hold products (read *toys*). When we cater to their whims, we rob them of wishing and reinforce their role as consumers. We actually contribute to their self-involvement.

"Parents who give their children everything shouldn't complain that their kids are spoiled."[2]

THE QUEST FOR COMFORT

Princesses and princes expect to be treated well. Not only do they expect the best stuff, they expect comfort. Far be it from them to have to "rough it" for a while.

Delayed gratification is something for other people. By the time our children become young adults, they are material-oriented; we have done them a great disservice. In *Boomerang Kids*, Jean Okimoto and Phyllis Stegall summarize the outcome of this quest for comfort and possessions:

> The young adults of today have spent many formative and impressionable years in a society that worshiped "the right stuff," not the stuff of character, but things, things, and more things: the right label, the right brand, the right make, the right model, the right name, *the right stuff*. Consumerism and materialism have caused many young adults to covet a designer life-style.[3]

The passion for a designer life-style, coupled with a sense of entitlement, has made many of our kids into princesses and princes. They have inherited comfort as a minimum standard.

For many young adults, the "designer life-style" isn't affordable. Yet they feel the pressure to acquire and succeed quickly.

The pressure leads to unrealistic expectations. If they cannot support their lifestyle with their present paycheck, what can they do? The answer is they rush into the wonderful world of easy credit.

When the bills come due, reality comes crashing in. Their upwardly mobile tastes aren't supported by their downwardly mobile income. Some get wise and cut back purchases and simplify their lifestyle. Some try to consolidate and they live on their own; but others move back home, trying to maintain some semblance of their lifestyle. Parents let them come home "to save money."

WATCH OUT FOR THE "BOOMERANG KIDS"

Grown-up children who return home to live with parents have been tagged the "Boomerang Kids." I remember one striking TV report on this phenomenon. One of the young men interviewed was a successful twenty-seven-year-old attorney who had moved back home. As a single man, he had it made. His parents lived in a million-dollar home with a swimming pool, tennis court, and four-car garage. And he brought home $100,000 a year!

Not all adult children at home earn such an income, of course. Yet many grown-up children have sufficient income to live on their own, though they may need to reduce their level of comfort. Still parents let them return home to maintain a level of comfort with which they grew up. In doing so, we parents have created a kind of entitlement for our children. "I had it before. I deserve it." We have created a generation of the privileged. Entitlement has become the paradigm for many of today's youth. As a result, we create disadvantaged children of plenty.

WHY PARENTS PRODUCE PRINCES AND PRINCESSES

To Keep Them from "Struggling"

What causes us to produce princes and princesses? I think it has to do with well-intentioned parents who do too much, or demand too little. We often do not want them to struggle. Ironically, when we supply their every want, we insulate them against the very things that would make them stronger.

The issue is indulgence, a luxury that previous generations never had. They were too busy surviving the Depression, or fighting a war. But our expectations for ourselves and our children have changed. We grew up viewing TV families where the child was the center of focus. Supply his needs, give him what he wants. A new kind of scientist, called a *psychologist*, informed parents of the complex "needs" of the child, "needs" not known to previous generations. Now, parents were to build their lives around meeting their child's needs. A good parent would make it his top priority.

To Meet Their Needs—and Wants

The requirements for being a good parent have increased. Prior to the 1960s, they were obvious and simple. Being a good dad meant being a good provider. Bring home the paycheck. Provide food, shelter, and clothing. Being a good mom meant keeping the house, washing the clothes, cooking three meals a day, and not working outside the home.

But in the 1960s we experienced a revolution. The Revolution of The Child.

Families became child-centric. The kids became the hub of the attention and activity. Parents wanted their kids to feel good about themselves, to have their wants met, and to blossom with creative expression.

To Keep Them from Failure

Parents didn't want their kids to experience failure. As a result, many parents lobbied for change in public education. They marched to the schools and mandated that their children learn in an "open classroom." That they "learn at their own pace." Between well-intentioned parents and liberal education proponents, "flunking" was thrown out the door for the more trendy, and sensitive, "Pass-Fail" approach. If a child somehow got out of step with the learning, parents begged for a "special project" for "extra credit." Parents then worked hours, as their children watched, to produce a project worthy of the bail-out credit. Children were never supposed to experience failure.

The outcome was that these children never really understood the reality of consequences. With someone always available to bail them out, these kids were denied the opportunity to solve problems on their own. In an effort to help, parents deprived their kids the growth that can come only by facing adversity. Instead of feeling confident about themselves, they became unsure, dependent, and fragile. They resented their parents, but they needed them. And our children began to believe they were, indeed, the center of the universe, deserving of having everything and undeserving of setbacks in life.

> In the middle of all this activity, something happened within the head of The Child. The Child got the idea that he or she was indeed *The Center Of The Universe*. Unfortunately, this feeling does not help one adapt to a real world filled with setbacks, disappointments, consequences, and losses, a world where people get evicted from apartments, fired from jobs, and dumped in relationships. The mind-set of the depression-era generation, when life was *expected* to be a struggle, actually equipped its young adults much better for life in the real world.
>
> Feeling that one is the center of the universe also does not prepare a person to meet the demands of an intimate relationship, which requires compromise, negotiation, an extraordinary capacity to give, and caring as deeply for another as one does for oneself.[4]

Relaxed parents will not give their children everything. Rather than worry about their children being deprived of certain items and being exposed to some hardship, we should feel confident in how we raise our children. We should even recognize that some difficulty and discomfort is good for our children—just as it is for us. Beyond building our children's character, it helps parents and children work as a family to make do with what is available.

DISADVANTAGED CHILDREN OF PLENTY

Making it too easy for our kids can make them weak. If we rescue them from all adversity, we are only reinforcing their expectation that they deserve to be comfortable and have all of their wants met. And that's unrealistic. They will never have their every want met. Gosman calls the desire that our children feel good an unhealthy obsession:

> Our obsession with our children's feeling good is simply not producing children who feel good. We parents need to take our kids off their pedestals, be more accepting and forgiving of ourselves and more demanding of them. We need to realize that effective, reasonable discipline is as much a part of love as hugs and kisses. . . . Our children . . . desperately need to learn that life is not pain-free, and that disappointments, sacrifices, and occasional failures are as much a part of life as party favors, soccer camps, and Nintendo.[5]

Gosman is right. It's time to take the prince and princess off the pedestal. Instead of handing them a pillow, we need to hand them a rake. I have actually observed some children do yard work in their own yards! Sadly, for some children, the biggest challenge they have in a day is trying to get to the next level playing Mario Brothers video game.

Here's a novel concept: *Parents are in charge!* Homes aren't democracies. Not everyone has an equal say. Children aren't our equals, possessing equal rights and privileges. They are children. Families should be run by parents, not children. We don't have to give our children everything they think they "need." We can actually say "no." Practice it right now. Repeat after me, "No." Again, "No." Feels good, doesn't it? One more time, "No." Now that you can say it, use it.

Clearly we can and must learn to say no to our children's wants while taking care of their needs. But that raises a key question: How can we distinguish between wants and needs?

Here are a couple of simple definitions. *Needs* are basic biological needs; *wants* are everything else our children desire. Needs include food, water, and air—along with a reasonable amount of attention, affection, intellectual and physical stimulation, and opportunities to be competent. Those needs are a priority; we should satisfy needs as quickly as possible. But remember, everything else our kids desire is a *want*, whether it is something to eat, a material object, or getting their own way. Some wants should not be satisfied at all. Other wants may be reasonable, but not satisfied on demand. Make them earn or wait for them. This helps kids delay gratification and focus on internal values.[6]

FEELINGS OF ENTITLEMENT: "I DESERVE IT!

Pampered princesses. Self-centered princes. Don't worry, it's not all your fault. You had help. I call it *The Curse of Mr. Rogers.* Yeah, that's right, Mr. Rogers, the guy on public television with the cozy neighborhood. It's not the sweater that did it. Not the changing of the shoes. Not even that fake, little train and town scene. It's the idea that "you are _____." You know the word. You have heard the rhetoric, "There is no one like you. You are the only you. You are *special.*"

If kids grow up hearing they are special, they begin to feel they are entitled to have everything they want. Each individual is important. But often the message gets distracted and kids think they are better than others. And it becomes the breeding ground for self-centeredness. I know that's not what Mr. Rogers intended. And it's not his fault alone. The "you are special" movement is everywhere, and in announcing its message, the movement has failed to remind children and parents alike that others are special, too. And we must help others, not just ourselves. When kids grow up with an emphasis on individuality apart from responsibility, they develop the perspective that they are "just a little better" than others because "they are special."

How can *everyone* be special?

"Good morning, students, and welcome to Meadow School. I am Principal Finkerbean. At Meadow School we consider each student to be special. Each is a pretty flower. No two flowers are alike. Each student is like a snowflake. You are different. You are unique. You are special. We are here to help you feel good about yourself. To help you discover your own beauty as a flower. Your own identity as a snowflake—your snowflakeness. You are the only 'you' you will ever know. You need to know 'you.' You need to feel good about 'you.' Join us in this discovery! Now, go to class."

WATCH OUT FOR NARCISSISM

An emphasis on individuality apart from community produces narcissism. We've produced self-involved children because we didn't tell them the whole story. Individuals are important for what they can contribute to the community. Not for their inherently distinctive individuality. Such children "never felt that they had a role to play in the community or the family, and certainly never believed that they might have to sacrifice their individuality."[7]

Humanism has successfully affirmed individuality. But the pendulum has swung too far. We have an entire generation bent on "doing their own thing." We need to see a balance towards affirming community. We need to hear "You are special because of your individual responsibility."

The chorus for individuality has been sung. Its lyrics repeat, "What can I *get?*" Harmony calls for singing the other part—the part of community. Its lyrics ask, "What can I *give?*"

Individuality needs to be affirmed in the context of community. Individuals need to be affirmed for their role and contribution to the family. This makes each person a contributing, responsible member. Families have members, not guests.

There are many ways to make our children into princes and princesses. Spoiling them is only one way. If our child isn't effectively disciplined for misbehavior, then he is spoiled. If her mediocre effort is tolerated, then she is spoiled. If his opinions are unreasonably deferred to, then he is spoiled. If she isn't held responsible for her actions, then she is spoiled.[8]

Relaxed parents will treat their children as members of the family, not as guests. Their children have duties to a household and eventually to a community. Children deserve to have their needs cared for, but relaxed parents are comfortable not giving in to their children's every want. Relaxed parents care enough and are confident enough to let their children face struggles and do without the unessential. They know that's the best way to prepare their children to be mature adults who can accept hardship and loss in life.

Reflections

FOR THE RELAXED PARENT

1. What do you think about Jose's gifts to his children?
2. "Just because you can afford to give your child something doesn't mean you should." Do you agree/disagree? Why?
3. Do you think children are losing the benefits of waiting and anticipation?
4. How do you keep your child from expecting comfort as a standard?
5. In your experience, have you met youth who have feelings of entitlement, who say, "I'm entitled to this"?
6. What are some ways we put our children up on a pedestal?
7. What would happen in your family if you were to adopt the motto: "Families have members, not guests"?

Skill Builder

CLUB FAMILY

Imagine your family is a club. Each person is a valuable and contributing member. As in any club, there are dues to pay and officers who are in charge. Each person has a role and a responsibility. Discuss what it would be like. Your club can be located anywhere you wish. But you must all agree on the location, the name, and the purpose of the club.

Try to assign a job and a uniform for each family member.

What would happen if one or more members began to act like guests and not contributing members?

$\mathcal{P}$ARENTING $\mathcal{P}$RINCIPLE

The relaxed parent chooses to not give children too much, recognizing to do so may be giving them too little.

Six

SPOILED-ROTTEN KIDS

*T*his is boring!" shouted twelve-year-old Daniel in front of seventy-five other junior high students.

I had been directing the evening club program for junior high students. The teens had begun the night with a creative crowd breaker, followed by a highly physical game. Then they watched an MTV-quality video on a relevant topic, followed by small groups to allow students to share their opinions. The evening was coming to a close with a five-minute humorous talk on friends. Every eight minutes we did something different, but all related to the theme on friends. I thought it was an innovative program.

"This is boooring!" shouted Daniel again.

My first reaction was to punch him out. I held back—reluctantly. Our staff had worked for hours to pull this program together, and this eighty-pound mouth was declaring it worthless.

I'd like to teach him a lesson on respect! I thought.

I wasn't sure what to do. Never had a student interrupted me with a shout to announce that what I was saying was boring. I was so angry, I decided not to respond. I was afraid that if I did, I might lose it and swear at him.

What would motivate a seventh grader to take on an adult in a position of authority? Who really cares if he's that bored? Since when is life to be entertaining 100 percent of the time? These questions racked my brain as I struggled to finish my talk.

"*This* is boring!" exclaimed Daniel again.

"Say that again, and you are outta here, Daniel!" I heard myself threaten. I should have said it earlier. Why did I put up with that behavior? Why does anyone?

Don't read this with that sneer. It's happened to you, too! We give in. We let kids get away with murder, or at least mayhem. Why do we give in to kids? Are we afraid of them?

Once again, I needed some answers. I needed some solid, objective evidence. I wanted irrefutable proof. I decided to do some serious research. Eventually I got over it. However, I did spend some time thinking about spoiled kids. I've met a lot of them. It seems that the more they had, the worse they were. *Giving children too much may be giving them too little.*

I'm not talking only about wealthy kids. I'm talking about indulged kids. I know of children who are terribly indulged by their parents who make a meager wage. The issue isn't wealth, or the lack of it. It's what we do with our stuff. It seems to me that we use our stuff instead of our skills.

WHY WE GIVE IN TO OUR CHILDREN

When parenting skills are lacking, we are tempted to give more and more stuff to our kids just to satisfy them. We give in. We give in to our kids for four reasons:

1. *As a substitute for time.* With both parents working, or a single parent in the home, the time demands are difficult. To compensate for the lack of time with our kids, we find ourselves giving them things or money. This helps reduce our guilt.

2. *To avoid a confrontation.* Tired and busy parents don't want a fight on their hands. It takes too much energy to deny our children whatever it is they want. The kids know that if they whine, nag, and harass, they will get their way. A parent reasons it's better to give in now, just to avoid the nagging.

3. *To compensate for our childhood.* If our childhood was too strict or too deprived, we reason that we'll make up for

it with our children. We want to treat our kids better than our parents treated us.

4. *To maintain our social status.* We don't want our kids to be branded with a "loser" reputation because they don't have the latest toy, fashion, or high-tech device. We fuel our own personal security through the "in" status of our kids and their stuff.

When we give in, two things happen: It hurts our credibility as parents and it sets our kids on the journey to becoming spoiled rotten. The relaxed parent chooses to not give children too much, recognizing that to do so may be giving them too little.

Relaxed parents not only avoid creating princes and princesses who have everything provided. Relaxed parents also avoid creating spoiled-rotten kids who get what they want and threaten parents with misbehavior if they don't get it.

TRAITS OF SPOILED-ROTTEN KIDS

There are good reasons not to raise spoiled-rotten kids. In my research (thinking back on all the spoiled-rotten kids I know), I have discovered twelve characteristics of spoiled-rotten kids. Read this list of attitudes and thinking, and you will see why spoiled-rotten kids will keep you from being a relaxed parent.

1. Feeling Bored

Remember Daniel? His calling card was "Boooring!" Why did he find everything boring? Because he expected adults to entertain him. He had a high expectation/low responsibility approach to life. He expected things to be interesting, but he didn't want to work at it.

Daniel is passive and critical. He is the classic vidiot. He plays hours of computer games. Life seems slow to him—no missiles, no lasers, no power packs, no points to score. His interest is visual and action-oriented.

When things get a little slow, it's your fault, parent! For kids like Daniel, their motto is, "What have you done for me lately?" Such kids have a constant need for stimulation. These amusement-driven kids are addicted to the rush. They haven't learned the value of quiet conversation or silent reflection.

2. Demanding

Spoiled kids want entertainment, and they want the best stuff. They won't settle for second best. Delayed gratification is as distant as the Paleozoic Era. Spoiled kids want the best, and they want it *now!*

The "best" isn't determined by actual value but by perceived value. The trendy, fashionable shoe is "the best," even though its workmanship is shoddy. Spoiled kids demand name-brand merchandise. Don't try to substitute a more practical purchase for an "in" must-have.

Eventually, knowing they can have designer-label fashions, spoiled-rotten kids develop designer tastes. And designer tastes lead to greed.

Since they have so much, they have little to aspire to. As a result, they crave stimulation and new amusements (the third trait of spoiled kids).

3. Addiction to Having and Doing the Latest Fashion

Because these kids are media mavens, they are constantly subjected to the latest fad sales pitch. They are vulnerable to the most influential media. They have not developed a filter to evaluate the deluge of messages they receive every day. They become programmable machines awaiting the most recent messages.

As a result of the media assault, kids are unified about what is "in" and what isn't. And the speed something can go from "in" to "out" is increasing. It used to be that music and fashion would cycle in annual revolutions. Now, thanks to MTV and other media, kids can know the trends on a daily cycle.

The ever-changing social commodity of what's cool and what's not really plays into the acceptance-driven child. The hot band on Monday may be rejected by Friday because someone saw a cool video by the new group on Thursday night. This pace of change, the influence of media, and the desire for acceptance make kids addicted to their peers' approval.

4. Lack of Sensitivity

Do your kids often seem jaded? Do they show they are sensitive only toward themselves or their own stuff? Don't worry, it's not just your kids. Many children aren't sensitive to the feelings and concerns of others. As they grow older and become more self-centered, children typically lack compassion. But this lack of sensitivity to others seems more pronounced among spoiled kids. Many have never been called upon to offer any help to people in need. Their parents either haven't explained the need to help others or, having explained it, have not given their children opportunities to practice it. Part of their children's lack of sensitivity comes from the parents having given too many goods. This leaves their sons and daughters unaware and insensitive to what it means to be without. They have little compassion for those who lack.

Several years ago I took a group of teenagers from Newport Beach to feed some homeless people in nearby Santa Ana. Though Santa Ana is only fifteen minutes away, most of the teens had never visited this area frequented by the homeless. Most had never been asked to help anyone in need. Anxiety filled the van as we pulled into the shelter's parking lot.

"Are these people safe?" one girl asked.

"Why do they live in the streets? Can't they get jobs?" a boy asked, half in curiosity, half in resentment.

"They are probably all minority groups or illegal aliens," said another. The conversations were laced with fear and prejudice.

That night at the shelter, our kids from Newport Beach discovered Robert, an eighteen-year-old white kid from Newport Beach. He was homeless, jobless, and hungry. I watched their faces soften with compassion. *Here's someone like us. This could be me!*

Later we talked about their prejudice and how we need to have compassion.

"He was living at home just months ago," admitted Chris. "He went to my high school. I could be Robert if I had the problems at home like he did."

I was surprised at the positive response we received from the students about feeding the homeless. This was something entirely new to their experience. Compassion and sensitivity to those in need was a whole new adventure for these kids.

Our children can learn to rekindle their sensitivity; they just need an opportunity. They need the challenge to be compassionate. Most kids still have a heart of compassion within. The wise parent seizes opportunities to develop this still-tender core.

There are many ways to do this. I know of parents who, as a family, have prepared soup and taken it to homeless people on a cold winter day. One family spent a week of family vacation building a home for Habitat for Humanity, an organization that provides inexpensive housing to those in need. Another family watched the video movie *The Diary of Anne Frank,* followed by a trip to L.A.'s Museum of Tolerance to help their children learn about the Jewish Holocaust. Exposure to certain experiences helps make our children more sensitive.

5. Lack of Self-Discipline

Spoiled kids tend to have little self-discipline. This can be seen in kids' patterns of incompletion. Spoiled kids like to take the easy way to completing tasks. If they want, they take the easy way *out.* Spoiled kids are easily tempted to quit. If the swim coach is too demanding, they think about quitting the team. And some do. If their biology teacher sets too high of a standard, spoiled teens want to transfer out of the class. If an after-school job begins to look like work, they often want to quit. Once the novelty and the fun wear off, spoiled kids have a hard time finishing a sport, project, or hobby. It seems like too much work to continue, and many spoiled kids want to trade it in on a different diversion—something new and exciting.

The root cause is a lack of discipline. They have not been made to persevere at tasks around the home—whether assigned chores or helping in a family project. So they lack sufficient discipline to stick to it outside the home. Because they do not complete projects, kids develop a general familiarity with many subjects, but no depth in any one. As a result, "familiarity breeds contempt."

I have observed that not all spoiled kids are quitters, but most quitters are spoiled. In their pursuit of immediate gratification, they have not learned the value of persistence. For some, their parents have accommodated them with a new amusement, never demanding that they complete what they started. Clearly, one way to contend with this lack of self-discipline is to encourage our kids to hang in there and finish what they begin.

Interestingly, a lack of self-discipline makes kids frustrated. Many endeavors in life are rewarding after a certain amount of learning and practice. Spoiled kids miss out on the satisfaction because many of them quit before they can appreciate any pay-off.

Are you depressed yet? Hey, we're only halfway through the list of characteristics of spoiled-rotten kids. If it makes you want to take a vow of celibacy and go live in a monastery, hang in there. I promise to send help.

6. Selective Truth

Spoiled kids expect honesty in others but not always in themselves. They may demand truthfulness in others, but for them it's "What works for me, baby!" In other words, they believe in selective truth. They want others to be truthful with them so they aren't taken advantage of, but they want the right to massage the truth to their advantage. When it comes to truth, spoiled kids observe a double standard. They want truth but they at times will practice deceit. Truth becomes a tool to manipulate for their gain.

For instance, some spoiled kid might become very upset if his parents withhold information from him. But he would think nothing of sneaking into an R-rated movie when his parents dropped him off for the PG comedy he had excitedly described.

Spoiled kids are innovative in discovering ways "to get away with it." Their tools include excuses, blaming others, half-truths, deceitfulness, and outright lies. Anything that keeps them from being held accountable for their behavior. Honesty is not a value for spoiled kids; comfort and freedom are esteemed.

Spoiled kids will fudge on the truth to keep their power. Convictions are secondary to convenience.

7. Problems with Performance and Competition

Spoiled kids can be competitive, but they seldom are good sports. With their parents' help, things have come easy. So long as they do well in competition (translated: have strong skills), they will continue. But if continued success requires more effort to develop their skills, they may blame someone and quit. Rarely do spoiled kids admit fault or responsibility. They have developed a razor-sharp skill of rationalization.

As a result, they often have troubles with performance. If a situation demands a high level of achievement, spoiled kids may wither under the pressure. Internally they are very insecure, because their entire life has been a series of rescues, starts, and stops. They seldom endure challenges or learn to successfully overcome them. Their fear of failure keeps them trapped in mediocre achievement (though they may think they are superior to everyone else).

Of course, as parents we are more concerned with preparing our children for life rather than a weekend game. The way to do this is to prepare them from the inside out, motivating them internally without having to make it a competition. The wise parent encourages his child to play the best basketball game she can, not to always win, but to see how well she can play. To see if she can make a major contribution to the team. The wise parent might say, "It's not just scoring points, in basketball; it's also making assists."

In chapter 11 we will discuss how to build motivation in our children from the inside out.

8. Focused on the Present

A lack of concern for the future is a characteristic of spoiled-rotten kids. They don't believe that the natural law of cause and effect applies to them. They believe that because they are special, they are exempt.

Consequences are not considered. The future is uncertain, so live for the moment. Spoiled kids live life like it's a beer commercial: "You only go around once in life, so grab all the gusto." "Eat, drink, and be merry, because tomorrow may never come." But in living for the moment, they are vulnerable to the quick, passing highs of drugs and alcohol. These modern hedonists either deny or ignore that addiction may be around the corner. They are just grateful that the substance kills the pain. As Donna Gaines noted in *Teenage Wasteland*,

> It is not surprising that the Alcoholics Anonymous doctrine advises never to let yourself get too hungry, too tired, or too lonely. Being emotionally strung out often leads to desperate self-medicating. The active alcoholic, overworked professional, and emotionally overwhelmed kid all appear to be wasted. Often, they are. Whether stressful life experiences or excessive drug-taking has wasted you is unimportant—a burned-out soul feels empty, the spirit seems depleted. For a bored, ignored, lonely kid, drug oblivion may offer immediate comfort, purpose and adventure in the place of everyday ennui.[1]

9. Lack of Purpose

Right about now you may be thinking, *This is a depressing list!*

You should try writing this stuff!

You may also be thinking, *Where did you get your list of ten?* I made it up. Not really. OK, kind of. Actually, I read several books on problem kids, spoiled kids, wasted kids, hurried kids, and good kids who go bad (like the vegetables in the bin in your refrigerator). I noticed a common thread running through all these books, and I'm not talking about the binding.

Kids who have problems have one thing in common—they lack purpose in their lives. As I thought about what these authors were saying, it agreed with my experience. Over the twenty years that I have worked with kids, I have noticed that kids with a defined sense of self and of purpose rarely get into serious trouble.

Kids who lack a sense of purpose usually find or make trouble.

In our age that rejects objective truth and moral absolutes, it's easy to lose our sense of purpose. If everything is relative, and nothing is morally right or wrong, then what difference does it make if I live? Or if I die? Or if I kill? American kids have had their dreams taken from them. Their vision has been blocked, unable to move beyond next week, because the world outside is simply too much. Suicide is known as the disease of hope. [As a teen, you feel] helplessness and hopelessness. Hopeless because you see no choices. Helpless because you feel that nothing you do will ever make a difference. You feel powerless and trapped. This makes you feel worthless; you can't defend yourself. . . . In killing time in teenage wasteland, some kids end up killing themselves too.[2]

Their lack of purpose causes kids to feel insignificant. They don't feel they have anything to offer. This fuels their self-absorption. Spoiled kids have no mission outside of themselves. Their mission in life is to focus on themselves. In time, it becomes a very fruitless and tiring obsession.

10. Difficulty with Decisions

Spoiled kids often have low impulse-control. They act impulsively without thinking through what they are doing. I know what you're thinking: *That sounds like all kids, especially mine.*

Spoiled kids are even worse. They lack critical thinking skills. They have trouble evaluating and prioritizing. These skills involve thinking in a way that is foreign to them. Evaluative thinking requires a standard for assessment. Spoiled kids often lack the mental "moral ruler" they need to make good decisions. They lack internal guidelines.

For them, decisions have been made with the immediate payoff in mind. Quick gratification is the primary standard for spoiled kids. Decisions are not pondered or thought through; they are usually made in haste.

Spoiled children develop a pattern I call "The Snagglepuss Syndrome." Remember the cartoon character Snagglepuss? When things got difficult, he would always say, "Exit, stage left!" and run away.

Kids often copy Snagglepuss. When things become difficult and require problem-solving and conflict resolution skills, kids are apt to run away. Avoidance. Lack of commitment. "When the going gets tough, the tough get going" is only a motto used in Western movies.

"What's wrong with these kids? Can't they make a decision and stick with it?" Maybe they have learned something from us.

> The disappearance of marriage as a dependable, permanent structure within which children can live out their childhood is surely the most consequential change that has occurred in the last two decades. . . . Children of divorce are made to understand in specific detail that their parents are often as helpless and confused as they themselves are. . . . They question: Who will take care of me if my parents can't even take care of themselves?[3]

The breakup of the family increases a child's vulnerability to the stresses of modern life. The concerns of the family often preoccupy the child's thinking. Perhaps this is why many kids have difficulty concentrating long enough to engage in critical thinking. Maybe their minds are on more pressing issues: *Will Dad and Mom divorce? Where will I live? Will I be with my brother? How can we afford two houses?*

This concept of perseverance is becoming alien in our culture. It flies right in the face of those parental tendencies that want to make it easy on our kids. It conflicts with the idea of protecting them from discomfort. It goes against the compulsion to have our kids like us. Being consistent means making a decision and sticking to it, against all odds.

It would mean not giving in.

It would mean turning the tide on spoiled-rotten kids.

I see the moon is rising. Time for the tide to change.

Reflections

For the Relaxed Parent

1. What comes to mind when you think of "spoiled-rotten kids?"

2. Are spoiled kids today like the spoiled kids when we were children?

3. Discuss the four reasons why we give in to our kids: (1) as a substitute for time, (2) to avoid a confrontation, (3) to compensate for our childhood, and (4) to maintain our social status.

4. Which of the twelve traits of spoiled kids have you observed in kids these days (not your own, of course!)?

5. Which of these characteristics brings you the most anxiety?

6. Why do some parents rescue their children from all discomfort?

7. Being consistent means being willing to have our kids mad at us for not giving in. What have you found to be helpful when this happens?

Skill Builder

BORING BOUT

Select a time when your children are a captive audience—for example, when you are in the car for a long trip.

Ask them, "What is boring to you?" Then see who can come up with the most boring way to spend time. Encourage humor and bizarre examples. The goal is to be creative and have fun.

The results may surprise you—or reawaken forgotten memories. For example, "I think the most boring time is when we visit Aunt Matilda and her retirement home and her TV is broken. Then we go to lunch and they serve lima beans, cauliflower, and gray mystery meat. To top it off, she invites us to the back of her room to see her collection of miniature pink flamingos."

Option: Anti-boredom Rx

Get a glass jar (like a mayonnaise jar) and some pieces of paper, about two by two inches. Have each family member write (or suggest, if they can't write) two or three fun ideas the family could do together to keep from being bored or to break out of a rut. Place the suggestions in the jar. Once a week take turns pulling out one idea and doing it as a family. Possible suggestions may include going to the zoo, on a walk, driving to an ice cream parlor in a nearby city, and giving everyone a dollar and seeing what fun outfit they will purchase at a thrift store.

$\mathcal{P}$ARENTING $\mathcal{P}$RINCIPLE

The relaxed parent anticipates the changes of each stage of life, and prepares himself and his children for each one.

SEVEN

THE FORTY-YEAR-OLD ADOLESCENT

T'm so sore from golfing, and at first I couldn't figure out why," Bill admitted.

I stared at his tanned, forty-something body. He was wearing his country club golf shirt, and it looked a little snug around the waist.

"Yeah, my partner and I were both complaining about our stomachs and backs hurting.

"Well, we finally figured it out. It's embarrassing."

"Can't wait to hear it," I said.

"Right when we started to tee off, this attractive young woman came up and asked if she could join us. Of course, we said yes. And she played with us, all eighteen holes."

"Was she good?"

"Yeah, she was great!"

"No, but was she a good *golfer?*"

"Yeah, she beat us both."

"So you got sore trying to keep up with her?"

"No. Fred and I couldn't figure it out at first. Then it hit us."

"What was it?"

"We were sore from sucking in our guts all day!"

The plight of the American forty-year-old adolescent. All across the country, millions of Americans are hitting middle age. In fact, in 1996 the first baby boomers, born in 1946, crossed the

not-so-magical age of fifty! Baby boomers are waking up to the
reality that there are limits to what we used to be able to do.

MIDLIFE REALITIES

Midlife can be a harsh time. Reality can be so cruel, and
midlife particularly perplexing. Someone has described midlife
this way. Midlife is:

- When you want to see how long your car will last, instead
of how fast it will go.
- That time of life when a woman won't tell her age, and a
man won't act his.
- That stage of life when all you exercise is caution.
- When the telephone rings and you hope it's not for you.
- When you stop criticizing the older generation and start
criticizing the younger one.
- A perplexity for modern medicine because it is undecided
whether it is harder on a middle-aged man to mow the lawn
himself, or argue to get his teenage son to do it.

Welcome to midlife!

But some of us aren't ready and willing to accept those
midlife realities. Like Peter Pan, we won't grow up; we are simply
forty-year-old-plus adolescents. I know some of you readers are
offended. "Why are you calling parents 'forty-year-old adolescents'?"

If the Nike® fits, wear it.

I'm not saying *all* parents are adolescents. I'm not saying *you*
are adolescent. I am saying that there exist, throughout the conti-
nental United States, forty-year-olds who are adolescent-like.
Those of you who are divorced are among those who know what
I'm talking about.

I was presenting this concept to a parents' seminar.[1] I had just
read some of the humorous midlife quotes and said, "How many
of you believe in this idea of a forty-year-old adolescent?" Half of
the crowd raised their hands.

"Those with your hands up, keep them up if you are divorced." Virtually all hands stayed up.

There is something about the trauma of divorce that brings out the adolescent in each of us.

However, if you're still married and have teens at home, you may be a forty-year-old adolescent too. There's something about the trauma of raising teens that brings out the adolescent in each of us.

HOW TEENS AND PARENTS ARE ALIKE

I have a theory. I call it "Adolescence Again." Parents and teens face common life-stage issues at the same time. Ouch!

Consider the physical issues. Teens are discovering that they are stronger and possibly bigger. Meanwhile, parents are discovering they are getting weaker and shrinking—or accumulating large deposits of muscle, disguised as fatty tissue.

How about emotions? Teens are experimenting with the full range of human feelings, often in one afternoon. Parents, too, face emotional issues. Fear, anger, rejection, insecurity, and performance problems. And that's before they leave the house for work!

Teens wonder about their sexuality. They are excited about their new "equipment." Parents, too, wonder about their sexuality. They wonder where it went!

Career and future occupy the mind of the teen. "What will I do?" "Where will I live?" "Will I get paid much?" "Will I be happy?" Parents muse over similar concerns about their career and future. Of course, their questions reflect their maturity. Yet they ask those same four questions: what, where, how much, and will I be happy in what I do?

Another teen concern is the family. Believe it or not, some teens actually think about their families. I know this may come as a shock to you, but it's true. At least that's what the researchers say. And, hey! You can trust the researchers. They work for the government.

Teens do have concerns about their families. Some are seriously troubled by them. We all are familiar with the myriad of troubles families face today. In these family concerns, teens are much like their parents.

There you have it: physical, emotional, sexual, career/future, and family. Each issue affects both teens and parents. Often at the same time, in the same house. No wonder there is conflict! Charles Bradshaw describes the contrasts in detail:

> The teenagers in the family are discovering sex in Technicolor, just at the time their parents are feeling a little gray. The adolescents are faced with an overwhelming number of career choices at the time their parents are beginning to face vocational change or stagnation. The adolescent's spurt often collides with his parent's mid-life reassessment—that critical time in life when marriages, careers, life pursuits, values and priorities are questioned, turned around and often drastically altered.[2]

In other words, there are two adolescents in most homes: the under-eighteen child and the over-forty adult.

Parents are often awash in their own perplexing search for identity at the same time as their teen. Take a minute and ask yourself, "What are some of the issues I am facing in these five areas: physical, emotional, sexual, career/future, and family?" "Which of these are similar to those facing my teenager?" Then ask yourself, "How do my life-stage issues and my teen's issues impact each other?"

I don't think it's a cruel joke. I believe it is by design. Right at the time we need to be available to stabilize and support our adolescents, we often get hit with our own adolescent-like issues. I think the Creator designed it that way to make us more sensitive and understanding. It's the old, "Walk a mile in my moccasins" idea.

WHAT IS ADOLESCENCE?

The word *adolescence* means "the period of growth to maturity." Doesn't that sound good? Take a break, get yourself a Diet Coke,® and ponder that definition.

"Adolescence is the period of growth to maturity." It sounds comforting, doesn't it? Hopeful, even. I like the word *period*, implying that this stage won't last forever. I relish the idea of *growth*. A rush of anticipation comes over me when I think about my teen growing to *maturity*.

Adolescents face changes physically, sexually, emotionally, intellectually, and socially. The relaxed parent anticipates these changes and helps his or her teen walk through them. The relaxed parent chooses not to be sidetracked by the externals: Your son may be six foot four; your daughter may look like Miss America; and the music they listen to may sound like cats fighting on a tin roof.

It does not matter. The relaxed parent focuses on the internals (rather than the externals) to deal with the change and challenges of each stage of life. At the same time, the relaxed parent isn't shocked by her own midlife issues, but seeks to understand them. She knows that change is an inevitable part of life, and that adolescence is a time of change for both the child and the parent.

So here are parents with a last chance to change their lives. And here are their children with the urge to discover who they are. Both are on the road to developing their identity. And their paths meet under the same roof. It's a meeting ready for conflict. But when you know what your developing sons and daughters are going through—what educational experts call their "developmental stages"—you can make the roadway smoother for them and yourself.

In fact, the relaxed parent understands the developmental tasks of teenagers, and makes a commitment to help her teen achieve them. The table on the next page summarizes the major developments your child faces during his or her adolescent years.

Understanding these developmental tasks helps the parent to relax and anticipate the adolescent changes in his or her child. The relaxed parent can model this spirit of anticipation to his teen. Instead of being ambushed by these changes and challenges, a parent can help the teen prepare for them.

There are enough surprises in raising teenagers. If we can eliminate some, it will pay off.

DevelopmentalTasks OfTeenagers

1. Physical

• *Accepting one's changing body and learning to use it effectively.*
The child comes to terms with the new size, shape, function, and potential of his or her maturing body.

2. Sex Roles

• *Achieving a satisfying and socially accepted masculine or feminine role.*
The child develops new and more mature relationships with peer groups of both sexes.

3. Vocational

• *Selecting and preparing for an occupation, as he or she thinks of economic independence.*
The child prepares through schooling, specialized training, and personal responsibility to get and hold a position.

4. Social

• *Establishing one's identity as a socially responsible person.*
The child moves toward a mature set of values and ethical controls appropriate to his or her culture, seeking to implement worthy standards in one's life.

5. Emotional

• *Achieving emotional independence of parents and other adults.*
The child learns to be an autonomous person who is capable of making decisions and running his/her own life.

SOURCE: Adapted from Charles Bradshaw, *You and Your Teen* (Elgin, Ill.: David C. Cook, 1985).

TIME FOR AN ASSESSMENT

As the relaxed parent, you may or may not feel like a forty-year-old adolescent. Even so, recognize that midlife is a time for assessment. It's a time of reckoning, and the relaxed parent isn't afraid to do some self-evaluation. I liken midlife to halftime in a football game. It's time to pull away from the game and ask some questions:

• "How are we playing?"
• "Is it working?"

- "Are we where we want to be?"
- "What mistakes have we made?"
- "What seems to be working for us?"
- "How should we play the second half? The same? Different?"

That final question is perhaps the most important one we each should answer: *How should I play the second half of my life?*

For many of us, our jobs have been our lives. We've worked for promotion and financial success. At halftime, many parents question the results. If that seems familiar, you are not alone.

Interestingly, adults on the tail end of the baby boom, ages thirty-one through thirty-five, are among those who have replaced professional accomplishments with rearing a family as their most important goal. A recent national survey of young professionals conducted by a national personnel service found that among ages twenty-five to thirty-five, 39 percent of respondents cited *getting married and starting a family* as among their most important goals.[3] These responses are in sharp contrast to the yuppie generation, which was chiefly characterized by consumption and professional ambition.

The survey, conducted by Dunhill Personnel System, Inc., dubs the new generation "Young Turks."

"Reacting to the 'workaholism' of the preceding generation, it appears as if young professionals will continue to focus inward, looking to foster personal satisfaction with domestic concerns, rather than making their employment the primary concentration of their lives," says Howard Scott, president of Dunhill.

"But no one's taking poverty vows," Scott adds. "A full 66 percent of Turks feel they will achieve a higher standard of living than their parents."[4]

A midlife assessment may reveal a loss. Perhaps the parent never found that fulfilling career. In fact, many younger professionals are recognizing this possibility and putting their eggs in more than just the career basket.

It is a dilemma. We want to provide for our families, but we want to be with them too. Our culture doesn't help. For decades we have sent messages that focus on career fulfillment. The intent, of course, was to affirm a person's value outside roles he or she was forced to be in—homemaker, mother, father, single parent. The job promised satisfaction; more than money, the worker thought she would bring home a sense of meaning. In some cases, this has happened. But for many parents, they succeeded at work and failed at home.

A DILEMMA: SUCCESS AT WORK, SETBACKS AT HOME

I have met some very successful people. Wealthy, articulate, educated, cultured, and respected—except by their kids. What caused these men and women to succeed at work and fail at home?

With tears in their eyes, they ask, "How can I be successful at work, and a failure at home?"

Parenting is succeeding in a different way.

In her revealing book *Children of Fast-Track Parents,* Andree Brooks noted that the skills, talents, and lifestyle that spell success in business and the professions can actually work against them in the role of parent. She analyzed the popular movie *Baby Boom,* the story of a management consultant who suddenly and unexpectedly becomes a mother. Brooks found the film comes to an accurate assessment of the skills needed for good parenting:

> Though much of the film is a satirical exaggeration, *it makes a powerful point: parenting can confound and confuse even the most accomplished individual* [emphasis added].
>
> In the old days the parent with the most highly developed marketplace skills—usually the father—was buffered by the mother, who had been encouraged to develop nurturing skills. Not so anymore. Both sexes are now urged to hone their marketplace skills. A woman's upbringing and training today may do little to prepare her for motherhood. . . . Many fast-track parents are thrown off-balance when they discover that raising a child frequently turns out to be more difficult and frustrating than succeeding in a chosen field. It may not actually be more difficult; it may just be that child-rais-

ing skills are indeed very different from the skills needed to succeed in business.[5]

What works at work doesn't always work at home. In fact, super-achievers rarely make ideal parents. Their single-minded focus on work keeps them from time-consuming relationships with spouses and children. Super-achievers are often highly competitive, and view people as tools or obstacles—even people within their own family.

"WHERE DO I WANT MY SUCCESS?"

The midlife parent has a plaguing question ringing in his head: "Where do I want to be a success: at home or at work?"

The good news is, it doesn't have to be either-or. It can be win-win.

You can be an effective parent *and* a successful worker. The key isn't working harder, or parenting harder. The key is learning to become the relaxed parent.

Take a look at the "Qualities Needed to Succeed" on page 100. What might happen if you were able to exhibit qualities needed to meet the needs of a growing child (those in the right-hand column)? Would you feel more satisfied with your parenting? Would you have less anxiety about your kids? Would you have more energy to pursue hobbies, or get in shape?

The answer is *yes!* In addition you would be a more focused and attentive person at home and at work.

The key is becoming a relaxed parent. The relaxed parent does not allow his worth to be determined by his work. She does not allow how others treat her to affect how she feels about herself. A relaxed parent is self-confident, but not afraid to learn, or ask for help. A relaxed parent does not look at his children as symbols, but as persons.

Forty-year-old adolescents may be in transition, but as adults they also can learn to adapt to their children and their own on-going changes. That's part of what it means to be an adult. And a relaxed parent.

Qualities Needed to Succeed

Qualities Needed to Succeed in a Chosen Career	Qualitites Needed to Meet the Needs of a Growing Child
1. A constant striving for perfection	A tolerance for repeated errors
2. Mobility	Stability
3. A need to be free from time constraints to pursue an independent life	Plenty of time for family activities
4. Impatience	Patience
5. A goal-oriented attitude toward the project at hand	Emphasis on process, surprises, and change as the child matures
6. A total commitment to yourself	A total commitment to others
7. A stubborn self-will	A softness and willingness to bend
8. Efficiency	A tolerance for chaos
9. A belief that succeeding must always be the top priority	An understanding that failure promotes growth
10. A controlling nature that enjoys directing others	A desire to promote independence in others even if their ways are not your ways
11. A concern about image	A relaxed acceptance of embarrassment
12. Firmness	Gentleness
13. A feeling that nobody is as smart as you	A true respect for your child's activities free from comparison with your own
14. A preference for concise information	Ability to listen patiently while children talk
15. An exploration of others	Ability to put another's needs ahead of one's own

SOURCE: Andree A. Brooks, *Children of Fast-Track Parents* (New York: Viking, 1989), 29. Used by permission.

Reflections

FOR THE RELAXED PARENT

1. What are some of the changes midlife parents face (physically, emotionally, sexually, vocationally, and with the family)?
2. Do you agree that parents and teens are dealing with similar issues at the same time?
3. How would an understanding of our own midlife issues help us in parenting teens?
4. Which of the "Developmental Tasks of Teenagers" listed on page 112 have you noticed your teen working through? Give examples.
5. How is succeeding in parenting different from succeeding at work?

Skill Builder

IN THEIR NATURAL HABITAT

Study the "Developmental Tasks of Teenagers." Choose one with which you would like to become more familiar. Don't tell your preteen or teen that you are researching this area. Don't be too nosy. Just observe them "In Their Natural Habitat," like those nature shows on TV.

Watch them for a week and record your observations.

$\mathcal{P}$ARENTING $\mathcal{P}$RINCIPLE

*The relaxed parent carefully evaluates
what he has inherited before
passing it on to his children.*

EIGHT

FROM GENERATION TO GENERATION

*S*hake your booty! Come on, everybody on the dance floor!" beckoned the DJ wearing the skintight white suit. A sea of John Travolta look-alikes from *Saturday Night Fever* started gyrating. Angel Flight polyester pants, double knit with flared bottoms. Tight vests on some men, unbuttoned blouse-like shirts on others. Gold jewelry on all of us.

That's right. I said "us." I can admit it now. I'm in recovery. "Hi, I'm Tim and I'm a former disco guy." Yeah, that was me in the white Angel Flight pants and vest. I wore double-deck platform shoes and my hair in an Afro (I'm six foot three with the Afro). Sometimes I would check to make sure my gold chain hung properly around my neck. My unbuttoned shirt exposed my jewelry and what I thought were decent pectorals. There was even an occasional hair on my chest, if I groomed it properly.

I was the 1970s' definition of macho hip. The disco I frequented was loud, crowded, and trendy. It was a surging sea of beat, tunes, and testosterone.

We were caught up in it. Maybe you were, too. We were committed to disco. We welcomed initiates into the pact, orienting them to the disco culture by teaching them "The Hustle." We didn't take time to evaluate what we were doing. We didn't analyze the environmental impact of disco. Our focus was on how we looked on the dance floor. You could call it shallow. You could label it self-involved. You could dismiss us as apathetic. And you would be right!

I'm not proud of it, in fact. But it is a part of my past. Not a big part, mind you, but it is a part. I didn't think it would ever influence my life in the 1990s. I thought those days of the BOOM-BOOM-BOOM had quietly slipped past and would be hopefully forgotten (like my student photo ID from eighth grade).

I sure didn't plan to mention my disco days to my kids. I didn't want to endorse what I did. You know, "Kids, don't ever do disco. You'll go deaf. There's too much evil in that place . . . What? Speak up, I can't hear you."

No, I was just going to let dead dogs lie. But certain things get resurrected, especially if you have kids. And so, on one hot summer day from my daughter's bedroom rose a familiar beat: "BOOM-BOOM-BOOM!" My music was blasting from my teenager's room! She was singing along to a Donna Summer tune. And she was doing it willingly, even with enthusiasm.

I thought teens hated everything their parents liked. How do you explain this resurgence in disco among teens? Maybe it's in the genes. Maybe she has a latent disco gene that is released by hormones at a certain age. I'm not sure, but one thing I know—certain things get passed on from one generation to another. From generation to generation, parents pass to their children habits, tendencies, and traits, some good and, alas, some bad. We pass on legacies to our children. (Could mine be disco?)

Inheriting a Mixed Bag

I told Nicole about my disco past, both because I thought it might be a common point of conversation and because honesty required it. Discovering her dad had been a disco guy intrigued Nicole. She found it to be odd and somewhat silly. She stared in disbelief at video movies from that era and asked, "You wore clothes *like that*?!"

"Yes, honey, I did."

"Ha, ha, ha!"

"What is so funny?"

"You went out in public and danced like that?"

"Yes, I did."

"Ha, ha, ha!" She was starting to annoy me.

"Well, we thought we looked cool," I explained.

"I like the music, but the clothes and the dances are hideous."

I looked at my daughter, who was wearing a baggy men's knit golf shirt and giant pants with a thirty-six-inch waist, doubled up on her thin waist. Her boots looked like rejects from the army of the former Soviet Union. Her outfit was MTV rap meets the grunge look.

"Just wait," I threatened. "What you think is cool now may look silly later."

I chuckled to myself as I walked away, humming, "Staying alive, staying alive, ahh, ahh, ahh, ahh, *staying aliiiiive!*"

We all inherit a mixed bag. Some things that are passed on are valuable: an appreciation for the arts; an understanding of finances; knowing how to take care of a car or which fork to use at a formal dinner.

Other things that are passed along are counterproductive, even damaging. Things like feelings of neglect or abandonment, perfectionism, substance abuse, and unresolved resentment. Those are things you and I would rather not think about, much less deal with. But the caring parent will, for his or her own well-being, as well as that of his or her children.

LEGACIES VERSUS LUNACIES

All families pass things on—some helpful, others not. Some healthy, others not. As parents, we may not be able to change what was handed to us, but we can influence what we pass on to our kids. We can decide what we will pass on to our children. It's up to us; will we pass on legacies or lunacies?

We are all too familiar with the lunacies. Perfectionism, resentments, and alcohol abuse are some of the generational lunacies that are passed on. A lunacy also can be as simple as a pattern of lying and deceiving workers, neighbors, or the IRS in order to look good or gain an advantage; children pick up on that. Or it can be as devastating as a pattern of verbal or physical abuse that leaves your child insecure and confused or bitter as an adult.

But what does it mean to pass on a legacy? A legacy is "something transmitted by or received from an ancestor or predecessor or from the past" (*Webster's Collegiate Dictionary*, tenth ed.). A legacy is a gift given from one generation to another. A legacy is different from inherited wealth, which might be spent foolishly. A legacy consists of an emotional inheritance; that's its undeniable power. So whether your children become rich or poor, with an emotional inheritance they are equipped to face life.

If you were to pass on to your children the certainty of your unconditional love, they would have confidence to take on life with courage. They would face the future with boldness, knowing both that they have value and that you are there, ready with your support. An uncertain future is acceptable, because they have the certainty of your love.

And so, parents, what gift do you want to pass on to your children? We must be careful, or we may give a damaging legacy of anger or fear. As Tim Kimmel has described:

> Children reared in an angry environment suffer lives of emotional exhaustion. Punishment without relief is torture. Families who fail to deal with unresolved anger are sure to passion their legacy to generation after generation . . . Children left with a legacy of fear are hamstrung when they move into adulthood. And the fear they've lived around may someday become the fear they live by.[1]

In chapter 4 we discussed how hostile and hassled youth are becoming. Some of this anger may be due to the legacy we may have passed on. If children inherit a weak emotional endowment, the confusion and hostility they face in their teen years will probably worsen.

Sadly, over time both parent and child accept their emotional torment as normal, something that comes with the parent-child relationship. One classic metaphor of a family member struggling with alcohol illustrates the problem. When a family is in denial about a family member's substance abuse, it's like having an elephant in the living room. Everyone works around the elephant, not talking about it, not trying to get it to go outside where it cannot hog space and disrupt life. At times, in fact, the family members are even accommodating it and cleaning up after it. The giant beast becomes part of their life. They figure, *It's always been in the living room, so that must be normal.*

A guest comes over and remarks, "There is an elephant in your living room!"

"So there is."

"Aren't you going to do something about it?"

"Why?"

"Because elephants aren't supposed to be in living rooms!"

"Oh, yeah? Says who? We've always had one."

"Isn't it annoying?"

"Nah, we're used to it."

What seems familiar may be interpreted as normal. What seems familiar will be passed on.

How do bad habits and crazy actions go from one generation to the next? Simply by watching and imitating those we love and respect—our parents. The action may not make sense, but we will think it does and may even invent our own explanation to make the silly seem sane.

Consider Sandra, a young bride who was hosting her first family Christmas dinner. She was nervous about everyone coming and decided to prepare a family favorite—roast beef with all the trimmings. The roast was cooking and the table was set. As Sandra continued to prepare the salad, her mother asked if she could help.

"Sure, Mom. Why don't you cut up the tomatoes?"

"Everything looks so tasty."

"I hope it is. I'm following your menu and recipes."

"Oh, I'm sure it will be delicious, then."

"I even cut off the ends of the roast beef, just like you showed me."

"I showed you that?"

"Yes, ever since I was a little girl, I watched you cut off the

ends of the roast beef before you put it into the oven," Sandra
said, with a note of pride and a fond memory.

"I didn't even realize I did that."

Sandra and her mom heard the noise at the front door, and
before they could put down the paring knife and long fork,
Grandma had burst into the kitchen.

"Oh, hi, Grandma. How are you?"

"Fine! Sure smells good. Your grandpa and I are looking forward to this meal. Do you need any help from a grandma?"

"Thanks, Grandma. Would you like to help Mom with the
salad?"

"Sure, dear. What's that I smell, roast?"

"Yes, Grandma. It's roast beef. And I'm fixing it just like
Mom used to. You know—her secret family recipe."

"How's that?"

"She cuts off the ends."

"That's where I learned it!" exclaimed the mother. "I learned
it from your grandmother. I remember watching her cut off the
ends of her roasts. They were always so succulent."

"That's right. I used to cut off the ends. You mean to tell me
that you copied me, and now my granddaughter is too?"

"I guess we did," Sandra declared.

"That wasn't some secret family recipe," admitted Grandma.
"I used to cut off the ends of the roast to make it fit into my pan. I
had a small pan and had to trim the roast to make it fit."

"You mean it's not a secret recipe!"

All three laughed boisterously.

"I've been copying you for twenty years, Momma. And I was
going to keep the tradition going, Grandma. Some crazy tradition!"

What seems familiar can become the standard, even if it's
cumbersome, time consuming, or even unhealthy. If it becomes
routine it often will be considered normal. This is how craziness
and bad habits get passed down to the next generation.

Generations pass along values, sayings, and baggage. Have
you ever taken time to evaluate values your parents passed on to

you? They might have captured a key value in a slogan or a favorite saying. What was one of your parents' favorite sayings?

HOW I LEARNED ABOUT DEPENDABILITY

When I was ten years old, I liked to tinker in my dad's garage. He had a well-organized workbench. Above it hung Peg-Board with hangers for each tool. It was the perfect "Tool Time" shop. Above the tool rack was a small sign: "The greatest ability is dependability." My father would often quote this slogan when he was lecturing me on "putting tools back in their proper and labeled place," or on the merits of working hard and actually delivering *all* of the papers on my paper route.

From my dad, I captured the value of dependability. I may not have all the skills that others do. Those may be beyond my aptitude. But I could influence a project with my dependability. I learned a major lesson from that sign, and from my dad repeating it: *You may not be able to be skilled at everything, but be skilled at keeping your word.*

That small sign above the screwdrivers introduced me to the quality of integrity. I have no doubt that part of my dad's legacy will be in teaching me to be dependable in completing projects and keeping my word. Similarly, your dad and mom have given you examples and advice that have meant help and kindness. Now, as the relaxed parent, you want to do the same.

WATCH OUT FOR HEAVY BAGGAGE

Great! But a warning here. You can pass along positive examples, like my dad demonstrating dependability, or you can pass along "baggage." I'm not talking about Samsonite luggage. I'm thinking of the stuff that gets passed on to the next generation that becomes heavy. You know what I mean. Things that carry history, hurt, and disappointment. Baggage is that tension that surfaces at family events. It's that tension that hits some families that are forced to be together on holidays. You know you have baggage in your family when you can't wait to leave your family Christmas holiday and get back to work.

Were any of these evident in the family you were raised in?

- Being ignored
- Teasing
- Perfectionism
- Avoidance
- Hiding emotions

- Getting blamed
- Overprotection
- Manipulation
- Secrets
- Addictions

If the answer is yes to one or more, watch out—you have baggage in your life that can slow you down. Some families have all ten of these. They might even be rules. You could call them "The Ten Commandments for a Hurting Family." They might be so common in a family that they feel normal. But they aren't healthy.

Part of being the relaxed parent is understanding the heritage we bring to parenting. As a parent yourself, the tendency is to hand the same dirty bags you received to your children. How can you end the cycle? First, realize that every parent brings assets and liabilities to parenting. Then be aware of the liabilities and develop a strategy to deal with them, a strategy to minimize our liabilities and maximize our strengths.

For instance, if you grew up being ignored by your parents, you might find yourself working long hours now to prove yourself. You want to succeed at work to gain your parents' approval. You might come home fatigued and have no energy for parenting. The kids become a nuisance. They are a drain of energy.

It's difficult to be the relaxed parent when you resent your kids.

Or perhaps as a child you were always blamed when things went wrong, often when it wasn't your fault. Now it has been transplanted to your parenting. At times you discover yourself blaming your kids for things that don't need to be assigned blame.

"Who left all this toothpaste in the sink?" you ask, yelling to no one in particular. "Why can't you kids be more responsible! How many times have I told you to wipe out the sink when you get toothpaste in it. If I had a nickel for every time I had to *blah blah blah* . . ."

Stuff happens. Everything doesn't have to be somebody's fault. Sometimes life is a little messy. The relaxed parent chooses carefully which safaris he goes on to hunt for blame.

A TALE OF THREE PARENTS

Yes, legacies can become lunacies. But we parents can change that. Here are three parents who found that their negative legacies meant they had some heavy baggage in the hallway closet. As you read these stories of Molly, Katherine, and Carl, you may feel angry toward their parents. But as each of these adults found out, the mature response is not to blame others and say, "Well, that's who I am now." Instead, they recognized the issues and developed a strategy to break the generational chain. And in all but one case, these parents broke the chains, and their children received the benefits.

Molly grew up with continual teasing. Her father was always making sarcastic jabs at her. After a while, it ceased to be funny and began to hurt. But it continued until she left home. Now, as a parent, Molly finds herself tempted to tease her children with sarcasm. She learned that teasing could be hurtful, leftover baggage that we bring into our families. Molly is working on becoming sensitive to not passing on this part of her family "heritage."

Sometimes awareness is enough to break the chains from the past. Other times, a real struggle results.

Katherine grew up in a very conservative, religious family. Her father was a leader in the church. Katherine was taught to obey her parents and stay away from any kind of "secular or evil influence." As a result, she had little freedom. Her parents wanted to keep her from being harmed. As a teenager, she wanted to have more freedom. She begged her parents to let her go to the school dance, but they refused. She asked if she could stay out past 10:00 P.M. after the church youth group outing, but they said no. At seventeen, she was fed up. She wanted her freedom. Katherine ran away.

Twenty years later, Katherine is a parent with a teenage daughter, Karen. At fourteen, Karen is already pushing the limits. Katherine struggles with balancing protecting Karen versus overprotecting her. She is not sure what to do. She has not resolved the baggage of overprotection from her parents. She has never really faced the resentment. They still talk, but it is strained. The conversation always focuses on the weather, their health, or Karen. They have never talked about their alienation. The subject is taboo.

Katherine struggles as a parent because she is carrying the burden that she brought in from her childhood. She's never taken the time and energy to confront it and be free from it. Consequently, she carries it around like an eighty-pound bag of cement.

Carl handled things differently when he discovered his generational baggage. He grew up in a home where his mother was very controlling and manipulative. She did it in such a sugary sweet way. But the agenda was clear—she wanted things done her way and on her timetable. Carl's dad went out of his way to please his wife, even if it meant going into debt. Carl's mom selected colleges for him when he was in high school. She said she would help to pay for her favorite one, so Carl went.

Carl's mom suggested he major in business and become a CPA. Carl did.

He didn't realize how his mother was controlling him until he got married. His wife pointed it out. He didn't believe it at first; but as he studied it, he realized she was right. At the birth of his first child, Carl decided to not pass on the manipulation he had put up with for thirty years. He was going to break the chain.

"Breaking the chain" means not to pass on the unhealthy habits we might have picked up from the families we grew up in. Breaking the chain means taking a look at behaviors and patterns which might be very familiar to us, and asking: "Are these helpful and healthy?"

AVOID THE AVOIDANCE RESPONSE

This is difficult to do. It's much easier just to ignore things. *Maybe they will go away,* we reason. Such a reaction is, in itself, an unhealthy way of relating. It's called avoidance.

Once you recognize the baggage, you must attempt to pick it up and remove it from your home. Don't ignore or avoid it. Lynn is familiar with avoidance. As a single mom she knows the cost of avoidance. It cost her her marriage. She was having problems with her husband, Brad, but she didn't want to face them. She poured herself into her work. *At least at work they appreciate me,* she reminded herself. *They're willing to listen, to give me praise and attention. But at home I get ridicule and complaints.* Lynn knew her marriage was heading for disaster, but she chose not to deal with it.

It ended with divorce.

Lynn came to one of my parenting seminars. She asked, "What can I do to break this pattern of avoidance? What can I do to face the issues?"

"Are you saying you want to break the chain of avoidance?"

"Exactly. I want to know why I am so alert at work and so out of it at home."

"You are wondering why you sometimes react like an ostrich and put your head in the sand."

"Yes. Why do I do that? I love my daughter, and I don't want to avoid her. I think we are in for some conflict. She just turned twelve."

"Do you feel totally drained when you get home from work?"

"Yeah. How did you know?"

"Because you aren't the relaxed parent. At least, not yet. Lynn, it takes energy to avoid. It takes less energy to face issues. You spend much of your day blocking out worries you have about your daughter. It drains you. You don't realize it, but by the end of your day you have had a slow drain on your battery. You probably think you are conserving energy by avoiding. But you aren't. You are only postponing."

"So it's better to make myself deal with it as it comes up?"

"Yes, the sooner the better. In fact, if you are at work, jot down your concerns and discipline yourself to deal with them that night. Make an appointment in your calendar like you would a business appointment. Your daughter is that important, isn't she?"

"She sure is. I'll give it a try."

Lynn was able to break the pattern of avoidance by keeping a weekly "date" with her daughter. This helped them keep current with issues in their relationship.

The relaxed parent isn't perfect, but she is willing to give it a try. She is willing to break the chain of habits which aren't healthy or don't work.

She is also willing to break the code of silence on family secrets. I'm not talking about confidentiality. We need that in families if we are to have trust. But I'm thinking about those families who have forbidden topics. Subjects that are taboo. They are items closed for discussion because they are hidden. If they were to be brought into the open they would be very embarrassing. Threats often accompany family secrets. "If you bring that up it will destroy your relationship with your father!"

To be free of certain burdens from our past we may need to bring them into the light. Into the present—into the truth. The longer we keep them in the closet, the larger and more powerful they become. I love that statement from the Bible, "You shall know the truth, and the truth shall make you free."[2]

Secrets can keep us captive. It's risky to shed light on old family secrets, but it can lead to liberty. The relaxed parent embraces truth. He doesn't run away from it. He doesn't need to spend time or energy hiding anything. He is authentic and transparent. No skeletons in the closet.

Sometimes we hide secrets; other times we may hide emotions. If we aren't comfortable with what we are feeling, we may choose to pretend. There are appropriate times to hide our true feelings and to accept the situation. For example, when you are a dinner guest and the hostess asks, "Do you like your liver and onions?" it's best to pretend. "I've never seen such a lovely presentation. The cauliflower and lima beans really accent the liver and onions."

Sometimes pretending is called for. We don't want to offend, and we realize the intentions of the host are good. But most of the time, it's best to be open and honest about our feelings. The challenge is sharing our feelings in a way that doesn't hurt others.

For instance, your daughter may be driving you crazy. She is pushing all of your buttons. You may feel like shouting, "You stupid, insensitive, selfish jerk!" I mean, you may really feel that way. And that would be honestly sharing your feelings. But that would be hurtful.

TELLING THE TRUTH WITH LOVE

We need to balance sharing truth with love. In healthy families we can speak the truth in love. We don't use the truth to beat up people, or love to avoid speaking the truth. We seek a balance between the two.

When we have a balance between truth and love, we have an atmosphere that is safe to share our emotions.

All families have baggage—things that go with them and represent the history of that family. When we unpack some of the luggage we may have inherited, we discover a lightness. We feel less burdened. We feel more free to be ourselves and allow our kids to be themselves. We aren't strangled by expectations and performance. We realize that failure isn't final. In fact, failure can be our best teacher. We begin to relax. And our children can be themselves, not what family counselor Norm Wright calls "a revised edition of ourselves."

We parents have the opportunity and challenge to be a "transitional generation." A generation that will evaluate what we have inherited from our parents before we pass it on to our kids. We don't want to pass on habits we need to break. We can be the ones who make the difference. We can be the ones who break the chain that may have been passed on from generation to generation. It's our choice.

Reflections

FOR THE RELAXED PARENT

1. Does your family have any "traditions" similar to cutting off the ends of the roast?

2. "What seems familiar becomes the standard." Describe how you have seen this occur in your family.

3. What were some of the smallest things that became your greatest teachers?

4. What are some ways we can "break the chain" and not pass on unhealthy habits to our children?

5. Describe how a parent might "speak the truth in love" and maintain balance between truth and love.

6. Do you agree that parents sometimes fashion their children into revised editions of themselves? Describe how you have seen this.

THE GOOD, THE BAD, AND THE UGLY

1. Take a few minutes to evaluate two generations, yours and your parents, using the following chart:

	My Generation	My Parents' Generation
The Good (something positive & of value)		
The Bad (something not to pass on)		
The Ugly (something hidden, embarrassing, or little known)		

2. Compare and contrast these elements with each generation.

3. Decide which of these to share with your child. Schedule a time to do so.

*The relaxed parent seeks to strengthen
the relationship with his children,
because he understands that not
every moment is a teachable moment.*

NINE
THE RELAXED RELATIONSHIP

*F*athers aren't getting the respect they deserve. There is a lot of dad-bashing going on. Dads would not get so much criticism if they weren't so male. I mean, being a male is a difficult role these days. We are looked to as the resident handyman. Is this recorded somewhere? Where does it say in the Bible, "Men: Thou shalt fix all that is within your house"?

In our culture, men are expected to be able to fix things around the house. Are we supposed to pop out of the womb with a tool box and a testosterone-driven comprehension of mechanical engineering? I think not.

There are other expectations for men, some of which are self-imposed. Men typically prefer the heavy work, so we volunteer for everything from lawn mowing to hauling boulders out of the backyard. We get a little embarrassed when the lid on the pickle jar won't yield to our mighty efforts when we first try to break the vacuum seal. We may feel miffed, our fragile ego cracking, when our wives firmly grasp the cap on the baby food jar and pop the lid that had resisted our big hands' effort to open it up.

Again, some of the pressures husbands feel are self-imposed. We drive for twenty minutes beyond a turnoff, not sure where we are but thinking we'll find the way.

"Why don't you look at the map?" the wife says.

"No, dear, there's no need for that. I know we're pretty close to the turnoff. If not, I'll just get off at the next exit and find my way."

So we take the next exit, driving past a gas station where directions are available, but we can't ask and look like we're lost. We proceed down the road until eventually we pull to the side and look at a map, muttering about road signs not being clearly marked.

The reason? Stopping and asking directions is a challenge to our manhood. We feel we should innately know a map of the world. It's supposed to be built into our maleness. As husbands, it's an admission to our liabilities and limitations. It's a brush with reality. *What happens if the word gets out that I am not capable at something?*

Wives, if as you read this you're thinking, *Well, of course, it's a male thing. They think they can figure it out. They want to be independent,* you're partly right. The main issue is our ego, for men are often afraid to admit that we, like our wives, are needy people who don't have all the answers. We're afraid of looking bad.

One other thing. We husbands know how to shift blame. It may be our fault, but it isn't *all* our fault. If they wouldn't make those jar caps too big (pickle jar) or too small (baby food jar), we could do it quickly enough. If the previous owner had taken care of the property, those boulders wouldn't still be in the backyard. If we had received clear instructions in our auto class, we would have properly removed the bolt on the oil pan, instead of dripping the motor oil onto our arms, clothes, and concrete.

DIRECTIONS FOR DADS—AND MOMS TOO

Let's see. So far our list of male things includes being a handyman, waste hauler, navigator, and auto mechanic. But since this is a book about parenting, let's add one more. Most men struggle with relationships—with their wives and their children. There are several reasons for this, but a major one has already been mentioned, a fear of looking "weak," of not having it all together. Of course, we don't have it together—no one ever fully does. But when it comes to rearing children and being a relaxed parent, relationships with the kids are very important.

This is not exclusively a male problem. Sorry, women, but you *do* need to read this chapter. Though women often are more honest about their weaknesses and more willing to talk about issues, they too need to learn how to cultivate relationships with their children. In fact, women are perhaps more frustrated about their relationships with the kids, since women tend to value relationships more than men do and so are more aware of incomplete relationships.

Relationships with our children are important. Done rightly, they will contribute to our being relaxed parents. Done incorrectly, we won't know our children well nor will we influence them deeply. Instead, we may find tension and misunderstanding in our homes.

The relaxed parent admits that he or she doesn't know it all. In fact, he's relaxed because he is not exhausted from pretending that he does. He's learning because he is coachable. He can learn from his kid.

OUR CHILDREN AS TEACHERS

The relaxed parent will stop and take time to process new information—for instance, stopping and asking for directions. He is not threatened by the idea that he is still learning, still growing, and still making mistakes. He doesn't need to be perfect to be an effective parent. In fact, pretending to be perfect would keep him from being effective. Fathers and mothers need to remember that they don't need to know it all or be able to do it all to be good parents and respected by their children. If you think that's the prerequisite, watch out. Children have a way of making us humble.

Children are built-in teaching creatures. When a mom or dad acts like she or he knows it all, the child accepts that as an invitation—an invitation to show the parent that she doesn't. When a mom thinks she can do it all, the child will research his mother's limitations and provide an opportunity to reveal them. That is childlike behavior. This is what they do.

YOUR STRONG INFLUENCE ON YOUR CHILDREN

The relaxed parent admits that he can't do it all. He doesn't have the skills or the time to do all things well. And that's OK. When it comes to having effective relationships with our children, there are two keys to being a relaxed parent: (1) Recognize that your influence is stronger than you think; (2) Your children want to have a relationship with you. Those two truths should encourage each of us in the up-again, down-again world of our changing and changeable children.

You and I can take comfort knowing that our influence is stronger than we think. Even when we "blow it" with misinformation, misunderstanding, and even failure on a project, our children will not disrespect us if we are honest and spend time with them. Studies indicate that involved fathers raise children who have higher IQs, are more socially responsive, withstand stress better, are more physically coordinated, and have stronger decision-making skills.[1]

OUR FEARS AND UNCERTAINTIES IN NURTURING

Spending time, nurturing, talking, and playing with your children are ways to shape them for a lifetime. Yet many men fear the idea of nurturing and touching. Many have never seen their own fathers model it, so they don't know how; others feel uncomfortable, assigning such acts as a "woman's role." But a dad's role of encourager and affirmer will never go out of fashion. Words of affirmation and encouragement from Dad will make a profound and positive difference in his kids' lives.

Mothers, this male fear of nurturing and complimenting may be affecting you as well. In my counseling, I have discovered many women who were never affirmed by their fathers. Their dads never accepted them as females. They didn't affirm their daughters for their feminine qualities. These women spend much of their lives searching for male approval. They have a hunger in their hearts for acceptance as a female. As a result, many women bring their own insecurities into a marriage, affecting their own children.

Many parents are not sure how and if it's necessary to affirm a child's sexual identity. While both fathers and mothers can play a role in giving their child positive, healthy feelings regarding his or her sexual identity, fathers play a crucial role.[2] Yet many men don't know how to express those feelings.

FATHERS AND DAUGHTERS

Three Ways to Affirm a Daughter

The issue of dads not nurturing their daughters is crucial, so let me give a few directions on how to treat your daughter. As a dad you can affirm your daughter in three ways:

- *Affirm her whole person.* Genuine affirmation gives your daughter a welcome sense of security and opens the gateway to healthy future relationships between her and you—and any future boyfriend. It is from her father that a girl needs to know that she is attractive, that her conversation is interesting, and that her creativity is worthwhile. If her father applauds her mental and spiritual attributes during her formative years, she will learn not to rely solely on shallow qualities like sex appeal to attract men as an adult.[3]
- *Affirm her ambition, achievement, and competence.* A wise father will convey to his daughter that these characteristics are not incompatible with femininity. A woman can achieve, and proper ambition is appropriate. A dad's confidence in his daughter and her capabilities will instill in her the confidence to survive on her own.
- *Affirm a balance between emotions and reason.* The relaxed father demonstrates an appreciation for beauty, for feelings, and for aesthetics. He also affirms reason, logic, and clear thinking. He compliments his daughter for making wise decisions.

I realized that many daughters never received this kind of affirmation from their fathers. I decided to do something about it. As a parent educator, I often present seminars for parents. Parents leave with a manual full of ideas. But on their way out, they often comment, "If only I had time to do some of this."

Thinking about this familiar comment, we decided to plan a time for fathers to spend with their sons and daughters. I discussed the concept with my colleagues. First, we planned a father-son camp out in the beautiful setting of Malibu Creek State Park north of Los Angeles. There we helped the fathers affirm their sons through a variety of activities: a low ropes course, recreation, and a hike designed for dads to verbally and visually affirm their sons. Some fathers prepared "monuments," small or medium-size objects that represented their love for their sons and affirmed them as men. We did it without screams and beating drums. But it still felt very manly—very warrior-like.

A Weekend Away

We also designed a time for fathers to build their relationships with their daughters. Several fathers and their daughters got together at a luxury hotel in Santa Monica. The daughters liked it. It was close to shopping and the beach. The dads enjoyed shopping with their daughters, recreation on the beach, and a special "date" with their daughters. In this father-daughter "retreat," the men met back at the hotel for a session on affirming their daughters, with their girls at their sides.

I was talking about how important it is for fathers to express affection and affirmation to their daughters. One of the fathers and his daughter slipped out to get a beverage. The hotel staff had set up a table with ice water and sodas just outside. As they took a break, a woman attending an executive seminar in the adjacent room also took a break and popped open a soda. Then, through the open door, she overheard my words: "Fathers need to express affection and affirmation to their daughters . . ."

"Excuse me," she asked the dad. "What meeting is this?"

"It's a father-daughter retreat," answered Brian, the father. "We're here to learn how to improve our father-daughter relationship." Brian motioned to his daughter, sipping a Coke.®

"That's wonderful," said the woman, smiling at the girl.

"Fathers need to feel comfortable with appropriate expression of affection," I continued. The woman was now standing in the doorway with Brian, listening intently.

"Dads, your daughters may need a hug the most when you think they want it the least—when they are teenagers! Don't pull back. Don't avoid them. Do what you can to connect, even if it seems like she's pulling back. She still needs you."

The woman's eyes began to mist. Brian noticed and moved closer.

"Ah . . . excuse me. Is everything all right?"

"Oh . . . yeah, I'm OK. I just wish I would have had a dad that did that when I was growing up," she sniffed.

Brian didn't know what to do. He didn't know what to say. So like most males, he stood there. I continued to talk about unconditional love and how much a hug communicates. I noticed this woman in the doorway.

There were two things going on at that moment: what I was talking about, and what was occurring as Brian and the woman executive listened in the doorway. The second activity was much more interesting than what I was saying.

After a few minutes of listening, the female executive turned to Brian and asked, "Excuse me . . ." She spoke softly, and Brian noticed the tears staining her cheeks. "Could I have a hug?"

Brian heard what she said, but he wasn't sure what to do. He turned to his daughter, still sipping on her Coke, and begged her with his eyes for direction: *What should I do?*

His daughter shrugged her shoulders, as if to say, "I'm not sure." Then she nodded her approval, as if to say, "Go ahead, I won't tell Mom."

Brian is a macho construction worker. This whole father-daughter-express-your-feelings-let's-make-a-sandcastle-together experience was pushing his limits. He was not comfortable. This request was really stretching it! But, with his daughter's encouragement, he decided to risk. He gave her a quick side hug.

I noticed it as I lectured.

The woman returned to her seminar. We found out later, she was one of the speakers. The topic? "Effective Strategies for Professional Women in the 90s."

Brian meanwhile had marched to his seat, but now he stood up. He interrupted my presentation.

"Tim, Tim! Excuse me, but I have to interrupt and tell you what just happened!" he exclaimed.

This better be good! I thought.

Brian described the incident, "And so she asked me, 'Can I have a hug?' So I gave her one. Was that OK?"

The room was silent with anticipation. Quizzical eyes darted from Brian to me and back.

Was this appropriate? Did Brian cross over some line? Did he mess up in front of his daughter? Will his wife get ticked? What will Tim say? They were thinking. Like most men, they weren't sure about showing compassion and care physically, with a hug.

I felt like the world was waiting as I thought for a few moments . . . tick . . . tick . . . tick. The anticipation was intense.

"I think you did exactly what we were talking about. This woman heard something that obviously cut right to her heart. It was a cry from her soul. She has a father wound. She really needed her dad to affirm her, and he didn't."

"So that's OK?" Brian feebly asked.

"Yeah, that's terrific!"

Fathers and daughters applauded.

Brian smiled.

Later on, as I reflected with a friend, I asked, "I wonder how much of that woman's pursuit for success came from her desire for her father's acceptance?"

"She sure looked successful." Observed my friend, "Gucci bag, Armani suit, and expensive jewelry."

"Maybe it's all part of her search for significance and acceptance," I mused.

"She had wealth, power, and position; but I guess she was still searching," he responded.

"A father's influence is more than you think. I mean she was just walking by the door and heard something that grabbed her."

"You're right," agreed my friend. "A father's influence is stronger than you think."

YOUR CHILDREN'S NEED FOR RELATIONSHIP WITH YOU

Your children need to connect with you. As a father, as a mother, you are being watched. From you, fathers, your son will learn what it means to be a man, and your daughter will learn what to look for in a husband. From you, mothers, your daughter will learn what it means to be a woman, and your son will learn what to look for in a wife.

It Takes Time

Developing such a relationship with your children will take time. Remember when you were dating? You took time to get together. You spent time listening. You discovered common interests. You shared experiences that both built dreams together and revealed the other person to you (and vice versa). You shared dreams and anticipated the future. These are the same skills that will pay off with your child. You still have these skills. Just dig them out, dust them off, and try them out.

Of course, time is also needed for dialogue. Take time to actually talk *with* your children, not simply *at* them. Discover their interests. Men tend to be more bottom-line oriented. We like to "get to the point." This may work well at the office, but it doesn't work as well at home. As males, our orientation tends to be to solve problems. Have you noticed, men, that this isn't always appreciated?

Sometimes our children and our spouses just need us to listen. Not to offer solutions, ideas, or answers. It's OK not to fix everything. Many times they want to connect, not correct. We don't have to be instructing to be influencing our kids. We can be building a relationship of influence.

Women tend to understand this better than men. Mothers generally understand the value of relationship. They may find it easier to talk with their child and not offer advice. For most men, it is very difficult. We have been culturally conditioned to be fix-it oriented. It feels real foreign when we focus solely on relationship and miss an opportunity for instructing, guiding or correcting.

About Those "Teachable Moments"

Most parents are aware of the need to instruct and guide their children, teaching them along the way. We can do this one of three ways: look for teachable moments, lecture, or have natural comments during our conversations together. But teachable moments, based on events involving our children, are not always available, and there are limits to lectures with children. But when we are developing a healthy relationship with our children, conversations flow, and during the dialogue we parents can bring up important truths and insights to teach and lead our children toward maturity.

The relaxed parent seeks to strengthen the relationship with his/her child because he/she understands that not every moment is a teachable moment. A strong relationship fosters good conversation and natural opportunities for the child to comment or inquire about personal issues and for the parent to respond naturally.

A strong relationship, by the way, includes expressing our feelings openly. When we attempt to honestly share our feelings, we show our kids that we, in fact, do have feelings—positive and negative emotions. In the turmoil of adolescence, our children may see that as common ground on which they can approach us.

Many teens doubt that their parents have feelings. They seem to view feelings like fashion: *Since my parents are out of it with their clothes, they must also be out of it with their emotions. Emotions are only for hip, cool people, not parents.* When we choose to reveal our feelings, our children are reminded that we have fears, hurts, and make mistakes just like they do. It can open the door more widely to a relationship with them. And such a relationship is the way to knowing your children better.

How well do you know your children? What topics of interest can you talk about with your son or daughter? Test yourself with the Skill Builder on page 131.

About Lectures

Lecture becomes less an option as your children move into their teenage years. Teens don't like lectures much; they're becoming independent and feel a lecture is a "control thing."

Some think they are starting to know it all (do you know the word *sophomore* means "wise one"? By the time your kid's about fifteen, he thinks he has most of the answers).

But conversations can help relationships grow. Conversations can help you pass on values to your kids. We want to have the kind of relationship with our kids where they pick up what's important to us.

> So much of life, in today's world, has to do with getting. Values, in contrast, have to do with *being* and with *giving*. It is who we are and what we give rather that what we have that makes up our truest inner selves. And it is what we are and what we give of ourselves to our children that will, more than any other force or factor, determine what their values are and influence who they will be and what they will give.[4]

When we connect with our children we influence them. We want to influence them toward things that are important to us. We want them to value honesty, courage, loyalty, respect, justice, love, and mercy. One of the best ways to pass on these universally accepted values is through conversations with our children. Not lectures, but dialogues. Ask questions, tell stories, play games, try role playing, and use imagination.

The relaxed parent knows the power of introducing values through creative conversations. He reinforces these values by praising his children when he catches them doing something good.

I emphasize the need for fathers to talk not because mothers do and dads don't but because men often receive little or no training in expressing themselves honestly and regularly in conversations. It's part of the heritage from their own dads and part of their own fear that disclosure will make them vulnerable.

Dads, you don't have to stay lost. You can pull over and ask for directions. It's OK, you are still a man. The relaxed parent doesn't try to parent alone. He knows when to get help. Yes, he can even ask his wife for directions! He can also talk with other dads about rearing children. The relaxed parent has more energy because he doesn't have to spend most of it pretending he's perfect.

Reflections

FOR THE RELAXED PARENT

1. Why do you think some men find it difficult to follow directions or stop to ask for directions?

2. What do you think about the statement, "The relaxed parent admits that he doesn't know it all?"

3. Which of the following do you think would be most beneficial in a father-daughter relationship? (1) Affirm the whole person; (2) Affirm her ambition, achievement, and competence; (3) Affirm a balance between emotions and reason. Why is the one you chose most beneficial?

4. How would an absence of any of the above affirmations affect a daughter? A son?

5. Describe a time when you experienced the maxim, "Conversations help relationships grow."

6. The author passed on values and concepts which were important to him to his daughter through letters. What are some creative ways you could pass on values to your child?

Skill Builder

HOW WELL DO YOU KNOW YOUR KID?

To discover how well you actually know your child, answer the following questions. Then have your child grade you to see how well you did.

1. Favorite subject in school _____
2. Best friend _____
3. Favorite kind of music or favorite performer

   _____

4. Favorite TV show _____
5. What really embarrasses your child_____
6. What really makes your child angry

   _____

7. What would be your child's ideal vacation

   _____

8. Most prized possession _____
9. Favorite place to eat _____
10. Favorite hobby or sport _____

PARENTING PRINCIPLE

The relaxed parent realizes effective communication with children differs from effective communication with adults.

$\mathcal{T}$EN

THE RELAXED CONVERSATION

$\mathcal{I}$ used to think of myself as an articulate person. I have a graduate degree and am an accomplished public speaker. Then I had kids.

At home, my vocabulary suddenly regressed to third grade and my logic became weak. My conversations included made-up words like *pooky, saggin' Huggies®,* and *cutesy-wootsy.* Having a child didn't lower my IQ, it just made me sound that way.

It happens to all parents. It's as if we all graduated from USC: the University of Stupid Comments. Parents have one thing in common—our kids prompt us to make stupid comments. Need proof? Check each and every comment you or your spouse have said to the children.

- ◻ "I have been worried sick; where have you been?"
- ◻ "It's all fun and games until someone gets an eye poked out."
- ◻ "If everyone jumped off a cliff, would you?"
- ◻ "You are grounded for the rest of your life!"
- ◻ "Don't look at me with that tone of voice!" (That's my favorite.)

Why do we say these things? It's scary, isn't it? We can be civil, in-control adults, with prestigious jobs, nice clothes, and cellular phones, and we can be made to say the silliest things by a twenty-pounder in a car seat—or a six-footer returning with our car keys.

THE MYTH OF COMMUNICATION

Usually we get over the baby babble after the first three years with our youngest child. But that doesn't mean we learn to communicate clearly with our kids. In fact, kids have a language all their own. I know, that's not news to you. But you may want to read on, for in this chapter we are going to learn their language— or at least how to communicate effectively with our children. Talking with children requires an approach different than talking with adults. Our parenting principle for this chapter tells us that effective conversations with children will differ from those with adults.

Now, there are books on communication, audio tapes on communication, and videos on communication. You can attend seminars on communication. But they won't help you to communicate with your child. When it comes to parenting, give up your fantasy of communicating with your child.

That's right, having an in-depth conversation with your child won't happen. Sorry to disappoint you. Like you, I once had a sweet picture in my mind: my wife and I sipping hot chocolate in front of a roaring fire, our children nestled around us. Everyone is snuggling. Polite conversation is occurring. People are respectful and considerate. Everyone works at listening. The topic is intriguing, and everyone is engaged in animated dialogue. Effective communication is taking place.

Uh-humm . . . Excuse me. Back to reality. Scenes like that only happen on TV. Unless you are Ozzie Nelson or Mike Brady, don't expect that to happen.

Still, many parents feel a sense of failure. We feel guilty when we can't live up to the communication fantasy. But I have good news. You can give it up. That's right, let go of your dream of effective communication. It's unrealistic.

I often ask parents, "When did you learn to effectively communicate?" Some responses:

"When I was twenty-three."

"When I got married."

"When we went to marriage counseling."

"After my second divorce."

Notice that nobody says, "When I was twelve."

Effective communication is an adult skill used in an adult world. Children and teens don't value communication like we do. They are content to talk and listen. They don't need to "communicate" like adults. That's why you cannot expect to have a good conversation with a child. Your son doesn't value it; your daughter is just learning how. When you do have such a conversation, treasure it for the rare jewel it is.

CANNONS VERSUS PISTOLS

One reason our teens don't communicate with us is because they feel outgunned by their parents' communication skills. I don't like to use military or adversarial metaphors, but in this case, it works. Parents bring to the conversation a big gun. They are skilled in communication. They have a fifty-millimeter Howitzer cannon. By comparison, their teenager is a fledgling communicator. His skills are weak. His experience is short. He brings a gun to the shoot-out. But his is a forty-nine-cent water pistol.

The cannon thunders, *"CAROOM!"*

The squirt gun squeaks, *"sitz-sitz."* The teenager feels outgunned. Family counselor Norman Wright describes the limits in our conversations with children:

> Communicating with children is different from communicating with adults. Adults enjoy free and open communication, but parent-child communication is limited to the understanding of the child. Adults give, receive and carry out instructions easily. A parent must often repeatedly remind and correct a child before instructions are finally carried out.[1]

Have you ever given any thought to how different adult communication is from kid communication? Let's contrast how we communicate with how our teenager might communicate.

LOGIC VERSUS RANDOMNESS

Adults like to communicate with logic. We communicate in a straight line: "A equals B and B equals C, so A equals C." Our conversations are logical and linear. That's the way we like it.

We also like to stick to one topic at a time. We prefer to stay at one level at a time. We try to not interrupt each other. We like to let each other finish our thought.

Now contrast that with teen communication, especially teen-teen communication. It is not logical and linear; it is random and nonsequential. In other words, chaotic.

Teens don't stay with one topic. They are comfortable jumping up and down to different levels of intimacy and vulnerability, sometimes without being aware that they've done so. They are comfortable interrupting each other or changing the subject.

For example:

"Tracy, could you believe it in science today? Mr. Dwelt is such a dweeb!"

"Yeah, he was wearing that sweater vest from the '80s."

"Get a life. Or at least a wardrobe."

"Hey, speaking of clothes, let's go to Melrose and go shopping Saturday."

"Cool. I need to get some new boots for the dance."

"Are you going with Kevin? He's such a babe."

"The hunk of the month is Trevor. Did you see him in P.E.?"

"I broke a nail in P.E. today. Playing that stupid volleyball. Why do we have to play? Who does he think I am, Gabrielle Reece?"

"Did you see her on MTV Sports?"

"No, but I saw the new video from Smashing Pumpkins."

"It's not as good as the one by Mustard Snort—it's hot."

"Gotta go—time for class."

"See ya!"

Parents, what you have just read might raise the blood pressure of most adults. Teenage conversations often seem pointless and schizophrenic. But they don't seem that way to the teenagers.

Adults have different expectations about communication than teens. They want to get to the point. In business terms, they want to know, "What's the bottom line?" But our children don't need a bottom line. In fact, they don't need any line. They are just chatting.

As parents, we often try to solve personal problems. We are solution-oriented. But our children tend to be more process-oriented. Just the act of talking for hours can be satisfying. No one may offer any solutions but, hey, no problem! They had a great time of talking.

The relaxed parent understands that a good way to shut down conversations with her child is to *try to understand too much*. Sometimes parents try to know all the details and have a complete comprehension of the facts. This can drive kids batty. They feel like they are being interrogated.

The relaxed parent also knows that another danger is *always seeking closure*. Kids are happy to leave things open-ended. There doesn't always have to be "a point." There doesn't have to be a moral or a lesson. There doesn't have to be a conclusion, a summary, or an application. Those tend to be parent things, not kid things.

A REVEALING ROAD TRIP

Environment has a lot to do with getting kids to talk. Many parents tell me that the best place to talk with their teen or pre-teen is in the car.

"We had to take a three hour trip to Bakersfield. There wasn't a lot to see, so we talked. I tried just to listen, and it seemed to work. That is the best conversation I've had with my seventeen-year-old son in years," confessed a pleased mother.

We discovered the same thing with a youth group I sponsored at our church. For years we planned what we thought were creative and fun events, only to discover that the teens thought they were just "OK." What we noticed, though, was that they seemed to enjoy the bus ride on the event. On the bus they were able to talk with their friends and counselors. For many, the bus ride was the best part of the trip.

As leaders, we decided to extend the length of the bus trip. "Let's pick a place that is an hour a way, drive there, get an ice cream cone, and drive back," I suggested.

We tried it. It worked.

Students and staff enjoyed their long, casual conversations. There were no interruptions. No phones. No pesky younger brothers. No nosy parents.

It worked so well, we decided to keep trying. After about six road trips, the students began to be a little suspicious.

"Why are we always going on these long bus rides? Isn't there something closer to home?"

We decided to not push it.

Why did these road trips work? Why do parents report that the best conversations occur on long car trips?

I think kids feel comfortable in a vehicle. They don't feel so out-gunned. They feel more empowered in a car. Why? Because at any moment, in any part of the country they can change the subject.

"Hey, look at the cool cow!"

"Wow, I've never seen a license plate from New Hampshire!"

"I wonder what they are growing in that field?"

"Are we lost? It seems like it."

Any of these will work. They are effective in changing the subject. They are creative interruptions. Driving has built-in distractions. Kids like built-in distractions. It empowers them for more equitable conversations. It makes things more fair.

PUTTING KIDS ON OUR LEVEL

Children also feel they're on an equal level during car trips because of eye contact—or lack of it. Parents are forced to keep their eyes on the road. They are focused on driving. This makes it feel safer to the kid. *Good, they're driving. At least they aren't staring at me with their stupid eye contact. I feel better when they aren't in my face.*

Kids are vulnerable at home. At any moment they could fall prey to the teachable moment or a reminder to finish a chore.

But in a car, they have some power. Mom or Dad is a little distracted because of the driving (at least we hope so). If Dad gets deep into a "teachable moment," and the child understands the point (or is getting bored), the kid can easily point at something and with animation yell, "Unbelievable! Wow! Dad, did you see that motor home? I think I saw (insert name of Dad's favorite celebrity) in there. Speed up and let's take a look."

It works. Dad presses the accelerator and catches up with the RV, only to discover an elderly couple and a Good Sam Club sticker. The teenager has shown his power, getting Pop to speed up, and has navigated his way out of a teachable moment.

That is why kids prefer to talk in moving vehicles going sixty-five miles per hour. A car is an equalizer. It is a safe environment that maximizes the water pistol firepower of the child to be a more equal match to his parents' cannon.

Try it. Take the kid and the car out for a long drive. But don't try to "communicate"; just talk and listen.

THE POWER OF CRAYONS

I was talking to a friend who works with teens about how to have an effective dialogue with adolescents.

"Teens don't value the same things we do about communication. They don't value eye contact, closure, and getting to the point."

"Yeah, I've noticed that," Dan agreed. "They are more stream of consciousness in their conversations."

"I found it helpful for them to have something in their hands when we talk."

"Like what?"

"A Coke, donut, any kind of food helps. Or skipping rocks across the water. Anything to relax them and give them something tactile—something to touch. It seems to open them up."

"I have two girls coming into the office for a counseling appointment," Dan said. "They are friends and they both are using drugs. What should I do?"

"Try taking them to a restaurant. That is better than your office. Find one that has children's menus. You know, the kind you get with crayons?"

"Oh, yeah. I know just the place."

"Get a quiet booth and start coloring. See if they open up."

"I'll try it," promised Dan.

A few days later I met Dan and asked, "How did it go with the girls at the restaurant?"

"It worked great! We went in and I asked for a booth and three children's menus with crayons. The hostess stared at me, and then at the girls' nose rings, but she gave them to us."

"What happened?"

"They started coloring as soon as we sat down. I mean they really got into it. I thought they might be embarrassed, but they weren't. Maybe it was because I was pretending to color, too. As Erica colored she began to open up." Dan then recalled the conversation.

"Yeah, I've been partying seriously lately," Erica said.

"Oh yeah? What do you mean?"

"Drinking, smoking, pot and . . . a . . . um . . . cocaine. Hey, can I use that purple crayon?"

"Sure, here it is."

"Me too," admitted Linnea. "But I'm cool. I'm not outta control. But some of my friends are." She nodded her head toward Erica.

Dan was amazed at the honesty of the two girls. Looking me in the eye, he said, "They told me stuff about drugs, alcohol, sex, parents—you name it. They really opened up. They were very vulnerable. The combination of the chocolate shakes and the crayons really worked!"

Dan felt he was able to give some initial help and was planning a second meeting with the girls, who also agreed to get help from another professional.

As parents, you may never have to deal with such serious issues. But then again, you might. It is critical that you are able to talk with your child. Sometimes just talking with our kids can keep them out of trouble.

FOUR TIPS ON TALKING

Here are four tips on talking with your child. The first one concerns your child's limits and was illustrated with the crayon story.

1. Be Sensitive to Your Child's Limitations

Earlier in this chapter Wright reminded us of the limitations that occur in parent-child communication. Such communication is limited to the understanding of the child. We can argue this, get mad about it, and even try to change it. But it won't change. Our kids have limitations, and there is not a lot we can do to change them.

We cannot make our kids into mini-adults. They have limitations because they are children. They have limitations with time. They can't talk about a topic for lengthy periods.

They have limitations with focus. They are easily distracted to another topic.

They have limitations with experience. Their library of experiences that help them interpret reality are minimal.

They have limitations with relationships. They simply don't have the network of human resources that their parents do.

Add these all up and you'll see that our kids enter a conversation with an adult with serious limitations. The relaxed parent is aware of this and plans accordingly.

2. Talking Is 50 Percent Your Responsibility

Occasionally I meet parents at my seminars who say, "I can't get my kid to talk with me! There must be something wrong with her. I fix a nice dinner, we eat it together, I ask her 'How was school?' and all she gives me is, 'Fine.' What is her problem?"

I introduce the parent to the 50 percent tip.

If you want to talk with your child, realize that you are at least 50 percent responsible. Don't blame your child for not talking with you. You have the authority and the experience that will give you a strategy for talking with your child. It's not all your fault and it's not all hers. Assume 50 percent of the responsibility, and see what happens.

For example, try to find a place where your child feels comfortable. Often this will be a McDonald's or Burger King—some place where she's gone as a little kid years earlier. As a parent, you can set up this time together. You may meet skepticism or indifference at first, but hang in there.

"I have an hour and ten minutes. What would you like to do?"

"Nothin'," replies the child.

"Do you mean nothin', or nothing with me?"

"Ah, well, I'm kinda busy right now."

"Too busy to go to your favorite place to eat with dear ol' Dad?"

"Well, maybe I could squeeze you in."

"Or you could spend that hour pulling dandelions in the backyard." (This is the part about the parent having the authority.)

"You know, a burger sounds pretty good right now."

"OK. Let's go."

The child then can enjoy her favorite meal in a place she feels comfortable. I think this tip helps parents relax. They know they aren't 100 percent at fault for weak communication. It relieves some guilt. The 50 percent tip helps parents back off a little. They know that if they give it their best shot, it still may not work. In other words, a parent's wishes don't magically become the child's. Our part is to initiate and create an environment for conversation; their part is to respond.

Some parents assume that because *they* want to communicate with their child, the child should want to communicate with them. Well, time for a reality check. Wishing is not an effective parenting tool.

3. Speak for Yourself, Not for Your Children

When attempting to talk with your offspring, try to lead your sentences with phrases like "I feel" or "I think." That would seem straightforward, but many of us don't really qualify what we say; we are trying to define and limit our children. When you are seeking to have dialogue with your children, don't speak for them. If you do, then they may feel they don't have anything to say.

With teenagers, it helps to be a little tentative. Instead of saying, "This is what I think . . . ," which the teen interprets as *I have to agree with Mom or I lose my freedom,* try being a little more tentative: "I think it could be a choice between option A and option B. What do you think is better? Why?" Kids like to give their opinions. We want them to learn to think. We want them to learn how to make good decisions for themselves. We can do all three in conversations if we present options and ask for their opinions. This helps them feel more responsible for their decisions. It also is an invitation for dialogue.

If a teen believes a conversation is just an opportunity for a parental propaganda campaign, then she will not join in. If she thinks her mom's opinion has already been formed, and there is no point in discussing it, then why have a conversation?

But if a teen believes you want his input, and are willing to listen to his perspective, then he is much more likely to converse with you.

Beginning your sentences with "I feel" or "I think" has another advantage. It recognizes that you may be wrong. In contrast sentences that begin with "You are (an ungrateful brat)," "You always (make excuses)," or "You never . . ." will kill conversations. They are unwarranted generalizations, negative, and absolute statements.

Try it on yourself. Imagine going in to work tomorrow. Your boss corners you and says, "*You are* not following policy with that account."

"But I . . ."

"*You always* are so creative at making excuses."

"What do you mean? I was just . . ."

"*You never* clean up your desk before leaving!"

How would you feel? Painful, isn't it? You would probably feel devalued. You would probably have some very strong feelings. You would probably have some very strong beliefs. Like, "I believe I will throw my coffee on my boss."

Here's a novel thought when it comes to parenting. Treat your kids like you would like to be treated. It's the Golden Rule applied to parenting: "Do unto your kids as you would have others do unto you."

4. Spend Time with Your Child

Don't fall for the "quality time" myth. You know, the parent who says, "We don't have a lot of time, but the seven minutes we

have each day are *quality* time." That may seem to work from the
parent's perspective, but not from the kids'.

Kids are on their own timetable. You can't rush them. They
like to do some things very slowly—like get dressed when you are
in a hurry and must leave ten minutes ago.

Quality time is a myth because it is a fabrication from the
adult world. It imagines that kids can act like adults. It imagines
that they can be intense, bottom-line, get-to-the-point, is-there-
anything-else-on-your-agenda? people. Which of course is, in a
word, *stupid.*

Quality time is driven by the need of the parent, not the need of
the kid. It comes from too busy, stressed-out, guilt-ridden parents
who only want to carve out a few minutes from their hectic schedules and somehow ascribe value to it by calling it "quality time."

Kids are like gardens. They take a lot of time. They take a lot
of effort. You can't always notice the fruit of your labor. But if
you skip the work in the garden, you will wind up with a jungle.
If you skip the time with your kid, you will wind up with a mon-
key, or a kid who acts like one.

I know this sounds harsh. I'm just tired of driven, compulsive
parents coming to me asking for help with their seventeen-year-
old who is "all screwed up." During the years they were building
a career, they needed to spend a little more time building their
child. Now they want me to help them fix it. Some want *me* to fix
it. They are willing to pay, too. But I resist; it's not my job.

It seems to me that some of the most successful people have
the most trouble with this. It's understandable. Wealthy, successful people are used to hiring others to do work that less fortunate
people do themselves. They have maids, nannies, chauffeurs, gar-
deners, tutors for their kids. But our children could actually
demand more time than what we have allotted in our schedules.
They often do.

What advice do we need to give this busy working parent?

We need to tell him to become the relaxed parent. Tell him (or
her) that he is working too much. Tell him to take it easy. Spend
less time and emotional energy at the office and spend some of
that on your kid.

Remember, no one at the end of his life says, "I wish I would have spent more time at the office."

THE DIVIDENDS OF MORE TIME WITH OUR CHILDREN

When we trade in the quality-time myth for some actual chunks of time with our kids, two things happen: (1) We have time to actually relax with our child; (2) we increase the odds for great conversations.

As parents, we need both of these, don't we?

When we relax with our kids, it makes them feel valued. Time spent with a person shows value.

When we have a block of time with our kid it increases the chances that we will have enjoyable dialogue. We need time to warm up to each other. Quality time results after we make an investment of quantity time.

The best conversations I have had with our daughters have been when we are on our family vacation or on a weekend trip. We have hours together: water skiing, hiking, mountain biking, going to the beach, riding in the car, or laying on the rafts in the lake. These activities are foundations for a great conversation.

Attention, all you overachievers! You are successful because you work hard. You are rewarded for your efforts. But at this stage of life, you want more than success; you have that. You want *significance*, right?

When you begin to feel significant in your parenting, the positive feeling will affect your work. It will help you feel more significant at work. But it needs to begin at home.

I don't understand it, but significance at work doesn't translate into significance at home. But significance at home *does* translate into significance at work.

I have talked with dozens of parents who were successful at work, but felt like failures at home. Their comments:

"Home is the only place I don't get respect."

"I am considered a leader in my field and a failure in my family."

"I work hard to provide for my family but they don't seem to appreciate it."

"If people only knew the real me, they would be shocked. I'm looked to as being one of the most successful people at work. I have lots of power. But at home, things are out of control."

My challenge to parents is: "Spend more energy at home and less at work."

Then home will become more of a restful, tranquil place where you can recharge, and then return to work with energy and enthusiasm.

The relaxed parent is a valuable worker because she knows when to work and when to play. To everything there is a season— a time to work and a time to play.

And remember, effective parents have relaxed conversations with their children by realizing that there also is a time to talk and a time to listen.

Reflections

FOR THE RELAXED PARENT

1. What do you think about the statement, "Communicating with our children is a myth."?
2. What do you think about the author's contrasts between teen and adult communication?
3. How does "trying to understand too much" shut down conversations?
4. How can parents reduce dialogue by "always seeking closure?"
5. How does spending blocks of time with your child increase the chances of significant dialogue?
6. Is it realistic to "spend more energy at home and less at work?"

Skill Builder

BLOCK TIME

Design a block of time to spend one-on-one with each child. Sit down with your child with a blank piece of notebook paper and your calendar. Then ask him or her, "What would you like to do? We have two or three hours."

Choose an activity that is kid-friendly and talk-friendly. In other words, don't go to a movie! Allow the preference to lean towards the child. This will help increase the comfort level and enhance dialogue.

PARENTING PRINCIPLE

*The relaxed parent has developed a strategy
to move from bribing to motivating.*

ELEVEN

HOW TO
MOTIVATE YOUR KIDS

*P*ossessions are just one way to spoil a child. Not helping her develop inner motivation is another. Kids are able to resist the lure of materialism if they have personal motivation. So let's talk about how to motivate your kids.

I know what you are thinking: *I can't even get my kid to do her chores! What is this talk about inner motivation?*

Parenting is the toughest job in the world. At work we can motivate people with the promise of a paycheck or the threat of termination. But how can we motivate our kids? Our goal as parents is to work ourselves out of a job. We don't want to be parenting our kids when they are thirty. We want to prepare them for life and launch them. Then we'll move to Sun City and take up lawn bowling.

To pull off this job we need to develop inner motivation in our child. But this is difficult to comprehend. What used to motivate kids doesn't work today.

I remember when I was about six years old, my mother would reward a clean room.

"If you clean up your room, you will get a Popsicle," she promised.

My sister, Becky, and I would work hard to put away our toys, take out the trash, and dust-mop our bedroom floors. When we were finished, we'd report our progress.

"Oh, your rooms do look nice," said mother as she gave the white glove inspection. "Here is a nickel to buy a Popsicle."

Becky and I went outside and sat on the sidewalk, waiting for the Ice Cream Man. Except we never could afford real ice cream—we had a nickel. A nickel would buy one double Popsicle, which we split. Remember the two-stick Popsicles?

Times have changed. Can you imagine trying to motivate your child to clean his room for two and a half cents?

What used to work in parenting doesn't work today. That's why every day feels like a day on the frontier for parents. And trying to motivate our children is stressful.

Well, what *will* motivate our children to want to do their best? I believe our children will be motivated when we work to build the internals of their lives. Watch out for just focusing on the externals. The externals have to do with performance and status. The internals have to do with character, integrity, and initiative.

THE HURRIED PARENT

Unfortunately, stressed parents typically fill their personal lives with a commitment to the externals—success at work, a social calendar that fuels status, belonging to several clubs or groups, obligations, and responsibilities that crowd out time to relax or be with the family. With our busy schedules and hurried workdays, we can begin to view others, including our children, as objects instead of people.

People under stress tend to see other people in the shorthand of symbols, not the often hard-to-decipher longhand of personhood. Under stress, we see others as certain obvious, easily grasped stereotypes and abstractions. We treat people as simplistic stereotypes because we are too wrapped up in our own illness, fear, or depression. Thus with our children; it is as objects or symbols—not as full subjects—that we hurry them. Why do people under stress recourse to symbols? To what end do they use them?

Basically, people under stress are not only self-centered, they also lack energy for dealing with issues apart from themselves. Symbols, oversimplifications really, are energy conserving. Parents under stress see their children as symbols because it is the least demanding way to deal with them. A student, a skater, a tennis player, a confidant are clear-cut symbols, easy guides for what to think, to see, and how to behave. Symbols thus free the parent from the energy consuming task of knowing the child as a totality, a whole person.[1]

The hurried parent has time only to glance at her child. She can't take the time to really know her child. She only knows a caricature of the child. As a result of too many commitments, she is stressed. She becomes guilty of drive-by parenting. The child notices her hurried parent. She notices that Mom or Dad fills the schedule with other adults and activities. So the child feels devalued and thinks her parent is too wrapped up in his own life.

The problem is typical for fathers, who derive great satisfaction and even identification from work and sometimes assume the extra time spent on job-related activities is fair, since it yields a bigger paycheck or paves the way for a possible promotion. But for the daughter, Dad's schedule implies he doesn't have time for her. Eventually she may copy her hurried father's behavior and become self-involved. She figures, *If Dad can't take time to focus on me, I better focus on myself.* She sees her dad fill his life with his choices. She decides to do the same.

Eventually this can lead to a daughter (or son) who is demanding, ungrateful, and critical. To curb her complaints her father buys her things. He has more money than time. He thinks this is a good way to show his love. She looks at the new purchases, but can't really enjoy them. She'd rather have time with Daddy.

Stressed, hurried parents produce spoiled kids. That's why it is important to become the relaxed parent.

Stop right now and think of the most stressed parents you know. Are their kids kind of spoiled? The parents need to become more relaxed, don't they? (Buy them a copy of this book.)

Character Development

In my mind, parents are either raising characters or building character. What does it mean to build our children's internal qualities? It means to prepare them for life, from the inside out.

It's more than teaching them rules. It's more than passing on family values. It's about developing our child's inner commitment to principle. Motivate your child inwardly—shape his character—and you will motivate him to good and noble outward behavior.

Developing a child's character has been described as a goal as elusive as reaching the end of a rainbow. But it can be done.

> The inner character of a child often seems as untouchable as the end of a rainbow. Perhaps that's because every child has a unique character that exists apart from any efforts to shape it. This fact is illustrated by a puzzle we've all observed many times: Children of unloving, neglectful parents sometimes grow up with a compassionate, loving character, and children of caring, compassionate parents occasionally grow up to be cruel and hateful. Despite this phenomenon, there is much about a child's character we *can* shape and mold. Unlike the end of a rainbow, you *can* touch the inner character of your children.[2]

Using Bribes

To build character we need to evaluate our incentive program. Many parents use the time-honored system of bribing. To an amazing extent, we can make our kids mind if we use bribes. Many countries have discovered the power of bribery and generate much of their gross national product through bribes. These countries, of course, are being run by teenage dictators.

So what's the problem with bribing? It gets expensive. Five-cent Popsicle treats don't work.

"OK, Dad. I'll wash the car if you pay me twenty dollars."

"I can take it to the car wash for less than that."

"OK. Fine. Do that. Can I have an advance on my allowance?"

The other problem with bribing is that it doesn't develop internal motivation for the child. It makes our kids depend on us for motivation. This is dangerous. Ask any parent with a dependent twenty-four-year-old living at home. The answer, once again, is to motivate from the inside out.

> Our goal as parents, then, is not just to change our children's outward behavior; we also need to affect their inner commitment

to principle, the values that govern the way they see themselves and the world. If we're successful in that, we effect change from the inside out. The child who has a personal commitment not to drink because of his personal value system will be strong in resisting outside pressure.[3]

HELPING CHILDREN MAKE
A PERSONAL COMMITMENT

I believe in helping children make personal commitments. I actually do it with our own children. In fact, I spent a year writing my daughter Nicole letters that would help prepare her for adolescence. I was worried that she might turn out to be like some of the teenagers I knew! These letters dealt with such topics as expectations, dating, emotions, friendships, substance abuse, and sexual standards. I wrote a letter, then we discussed it. I often would ask, "What is your personal standard on this topic?"

It really helped. I mean it really helped *me*. I was a lot less anxious after I wrote the letters. I think Nicole benefited, too.

These letters were meant to be our personal correspondence. I saw them as invitations to dialogue with my soon-to-be teenage daughter. Our friend Charlie Shedd had done the same thing years earlier with his son and daughter; his books, *Letters to Karen* and *Letters to Philip* have sold millions of copies. He encouraged me to submit my letters for publication, and the manuscript was published as *Letters to Nicole* (Tyndale).

I bring this up to shamelessly plug my book, but also to introduce the idea of having conversations with your kids about the things that are important to you. Or, as in my case, the things that are worrying you. Maybe you also would like to write letters to your young son or daughter.

That's one effective way to help your child make personal commitments. Nicole and I would often discuss one of the letters over an Egg McMuffin at McDonald's before school. It doesn't always take a lot of money or time to help prepare your child to make good decisions.

The beauty of writing to your children is that they don't have to listen to you lecture. They may even think that what you are saying today is pointless, but if you write it down, they may refer to it later.

It happened with us. I wrote *Letters to Nicole* when she was twelve. She wasn't too interested in boys and dating. But something happened. I believe it has something to do with hormones. When she first received some of my letters, she could care less about them. But later on, when she began to have "boy problems," some of my letters took on new life. She even began to share the letters with her friends who were having problems.

The past year she had a boyfriend with a car. Scary, isn't it? We began talking about dating standards. It is my belief that a person is ready to date when she has an understanding of the benefits of dating, the dangers of dating, and has written her own dating standards which she intends to keep.

INTERNAL VERSUS EXTERNAL STANDARDS

Many parents focus on the externals: "You can't date until you are sixteen." "You can only date boys we know. We also want to know his parents." Or even, "Your first year of dating will be double-dating with us." Such rules cannot create an inner commitment to principle within the child. They are external and parent-oriented. In other words, they will eventually fail.

I believe it is better to make it an internal issue. "You are ready to date when you can give me a list of the benefits of dating, the dangers of dating, and your personal standards which you intend to keep."

This is what I told Nicole. An hour later she presented me a three-page, carefully developed paper. It is a personal dating agreement. It is an agreement she has with herself. It has been my experience that teenagers are more apt to keep agreements they make with themselves.

Nicole has made an inner commitment to principle. She has her dating standards, and she likes this approach. At fifteen she could date because we thought she was ready. Many of her friends can't date until they are sixteen. This inner commitment to principle strategy is working to her advantage!

Such a strategy shifts your motivating factor from bribing to inner conviction. Building internal motivation is one way of building character. The wise philosopher Heraclitus (540–475 B.C.) stated, "Character is destiny." As a responsible parent, it is your charge to instill integrity instead of indulgence; to develop initiative instead of lethargy; and to demand compassion in lieu of selfishness. The ultimate goal is to grow character, not conformity. When we build character the result will be a lasting motivation instead of materialism.

Here are ten tips for motivating your child. Many parents have found these approaches very helpful. I heartily recommend them to you.

TEN TIPS FOR MOTIVATING YOUR CHILD
1. Allow your child to fail.

We rob our kids of their motivation when we always rescue them.

Sometimes helping our kids too much may not be helping them. They need to accomplish—and fail—on their own. Failure is a wise teacher, even if a painful one.

Parents often rescue their kids because they see them as an extension of themselves. Instead of letting them learn from the experience, they rescue them to keep them from pain. Thinking they are helping their child, they are actually robbing their child of his autonomy. The child is not treated as a separate human being entitled to his own independent set of achievements, direction, and failures.

Some of life's greatest lessons can be learned from failure. Trying to spare our children from unhappy feelings is unrealistic and unhealthy. Letting your child fail will let him see his potential and give him a sense of dignity.[4] Such failures are only setbacks; ultimately they lead to success.

2. Give your child regular household responsibilities.

One of the best ways to nurture a sense of family identity is by working together in the running of the household. When we ask our kids to assume regular chores, we are asking them to join a team. We are asking them to be participants, not simply spectators. Their emotions and work contribution are important and valuable.

When we affirm our children's contribution, they begin to see that they are needed and have something valuable to offer. This helps build their self-esteem. They feel good about themselves because they offered a service of value. We miss opportunities to build our children's self-esteem when we don't ask them to do regular household chores.

Tonight I made spaghetti for dinner. I asked Brooke to make the garlic toast.

"You are the Garlic Toast Girl. Make us some of your tasty toast."

She smiled and said, "OK, how many pieces do you want?"

She's not always that cooperative. But when it comes to spaghetti night, she is always willing to make the garlic toast. It is her place in the family. It helps her belong. It makes her feel valuable. She is contributing to our family. She also makes great toast. I know. That night I ate four pieces of garlic toast!

3. Decide to limit what you give your child.

This takes some emotional strength. Being a motivating parent is to risk not being liked all the time by your child. Remember, parents who motivate are concerned with what their children *need*, not what they want.

When we limit what we give our children, we help them appreciate the value of a gift. Our kids want all kinds of things. But they need a few essential things. When we limit what we give, we are teaching our children self-restraint. The lesson is: "We don't have to buy everything we think we 'need.'"

Saying no teaches another lesson. It helps our kids discover the value of waiting. Many times what was this week's critical must-have item is next week's forgotten token. Ken Davis calls waiting "a wonderful clarifier of truth." He adds: "Slavery to immediate gratification is the basis of many of the destructive experiences of adolescence and early adulthood, such as experimentation with drugs, premarital sex, and the bondage of debt.[5]

Teaching your children to wait, to say no to immediate gratification, will help them to develop self-control for their adult years in many crucial areas.

4. Teach and model respect for people and property.

If you want to motivate your children to care for other people and their property, help them appreciate what they already own. Help them learn to care for and value what belongs to them. Doing this will also help them from becoming ungrateful, possessive consumers as adults.

For instance, if your children want new bikes, evaluate whether they have taken care of their old bikes. "When I see that you are putting your bikes away, and not leaving them outside on the lawn, then I will know you are ready for new bikes."

Help them learn the lesson with present possessions; then entrust them with something new. This is simulating life. If we can't trust our child with a bike, will we give him a car? Will you get a promotion at work if you can't handle your current responsibilities?

When we teach respect for property, we are training our children to respect the people who own the property. Our goal, as parents, is to teach our children sensitivity. To show respect for the other person and his possessions. That means understanding the value of property so they won't steal someone else's or tag a school wall or bus stop.

The best way for a parent to teach respect for people and property is to provide an example. What can you do to model respect for someone? Here are four simple ways: (1) Be on time for appointments. (2) Be courteous with service people, waitresses, etc. (3) Drive courteously. (4) Don't criticize someone behind his back

Your kid is watching. Is he learning how to respect others by watching you?

5. Build into your child the value of completion.

Children these days have many options. Sometimes they have too many. They, like their parents, quickly become overcommitted. To help motivate our children we need to help them complete what they begin. We gain a sense of achievement and closure when we complete a project, when we finish an athletic season, and when we complete a series of lessons.

I'm concerned about parents who let their children pull out of commitments: children who tire of practicing musical scales, who want to quit soccer because they don't like the coach, or want to stop taking gymnastic lessons, even though the parents have paid for ten more lessons.

As a track coach, I've had several parents come to me and say, "My child wants to quit. I don't want to force her to do anything, so she'll probably be quitting."

"Track isn't that important." I tell them, "Life is, and the lesson they are learning is when something gets tough, or doesn't pay off immediately, you quit."

"Well, what should I tell her?"

"Tell her that it was her decision to go out for track. You didn't make her, did you?"

"No, of course not."

"Since she made that decision, she now has to stick with it. She is a member of a team and it will affect the team. In other words, don't let her quit. The big lesson to learn is the value of completion."

In several cases, the athletes who wanted to quit wind up having a stellar season—one that they would have missed had they quit. I know some of the other athletes who were allowed to quit. Quitting track was just one in a string of incomplete endeavors.

Again, the external behavior—quitting track—is not the issue. It's the inner attitude of *I'm not responsible to* anyone.

Sometimes our children think they can't complete a project because they are doing too much. They may be right. Help your child to do less so he can finish what he or she begins. Many kids are too busy with too many activities: multiple sports, music lessons, martial arts, homework, hobby clubs, and mandatory mall time. Maybe they would bring more motivation to an activity if it was the only thing they were doing besides school.

Help motivate your children by helping them be selective with their activities. Sometimes less is more.

6. Limit exposure to media.

Children are victims of the nonstop information coming their way. They are vulnerable to messages from all forms of media. They become overwhelmed. They are "drowning in information but starved for knowledge." We can help motivate our children by reducing the information overload. Incoming information requires processing. When children are overstimulated with information they become passive and apathetic.

Need an example? How do your kids look after watching four hours of TV? Energetic, active, and cooperative? Probably not; most TV kids become passive, apathetic, and grouchy. Too much exposure to media doesn't motivate. If anything, all the commercials create a lazy dissatisfaction with our kids. "I don't feel like doing anything, but I want to go buy what I saw on TV."

To raise your child's motivation, create time for him to daydream, to think big thoughts, to discover new ideas, and maybe even *read a book*. Limit exposure to video games, TV, movie videos, and online chat rooms. Each is OK in moderation, but many kids specialize in one or two and become passive sponges, not interacting with great ideas or even friends. Encourage them to have time daily to think and read.

7. Teach and model personal virtues over conformity.

There are certain personal character traits that are important to you. Make sure your child knows what they are. For us, honesty, faith, hope, courage, and love are very important. We want our daughters to live lives that reflect these virtues. These are more important to us than social status. They are more important than wealth. We want our girls to pursue these virtues more than popularity.

To be able to pursue such virtues, while others are chasing after peer acceptance, requires a child to be courageous. She needs to be willing to stand alone. Doing what is right is not the same as being exactly like everyone else. We build motivation when we help our child move beyond "sameness." She can be motivated because she is her own woman. She doesn't have to depend on the crowd's approval. She is motivated by what is important to her, not by what is important to others.

As parents, our example contributes to our children's commitment to virtue. A single mother at one parents conference told me after one session how she was trying to model personal virtue for her children.

"I work nine or ten hours a day and come home to a twelve-year-old and a fifteen-year-old who both want more. On weekends I need a break. I want to spend time with my boyfriend. Sometimes he'll spend the night on the couch. We aren't sexually involved, but it occurred to me that I wasn't providing a good example for my two daughters. So now he drives forty-five minutes home. I realize that if I want my daughters to remain sexually pure, I need to provide a model for them."

8. Hold your child personally accountable.

We've already discussed how rescuing can lead to an irresponsible child, one who depends on his parent to "fix everything." We hold our children accountable when we expect them to be responsible for their behavior. We won't allow their attempts at diversion or manipulation to minimize the fact that they are accountable for what they say and do.

When a child feels he can get away with misbehavior and not be held responsible for it, he will try it. He may try to blame others or deny any fault. The parent who motivates holds his child personally accountable for his behavior. This prepares the child for life as an adult. The parent who motivates uses consequences to help his child learn. He shows his child that there are always consequences for the choices we make in life. No one is exempt from the Law of Cause and Effect. (We discuss in depth the idea of consequences in chapter 13.)

9. Work together.

You can build motivation in your child by working together. I'm not talking about taking them to the office with you. (Aren't you glad?) I'm talking about working together on a school project, a scout project, or even a project around the home. Projects build relationships. A completed project, done with excellence, produces a sense of competency. It raises self-esteem.

Make a list of the projects that need to be done around the home. Ask your children to sign up for the one they are going to help you with. Explain how long you estimate the project will take and what is expected of them. Try to choose projects that allow you to be with each other and talk while working. For instance, sandblasting the driveway is not a good project. Painting the fence might be a better choice.

Work together on a service project. Teach your child compassion by helping people who are less fortunate than you. I'll never forget trips we used to take to downtown Los Angeles to serve at World Impact, an organization targeted at helping at-risk kids.

Brianna went with us one Saturday. She lived in a beautiful home near the ocean in Newport Beach. She was astonished.

"Why do people live like this?" she asked.

"Because they don't have a choice," I explained.

"How does what we do help them?"

"It helps to create choices for them."

"What?"

"By cleaning the school, sorting the clothes at the thrift store, and doing some construction, we are giving hope. With education, clothes, job skills, and facilities we create more options for them."

Brianna worked diligently all day. She went back home and told her dad of her experience. She asked him to help. He said no, and Brianna went several more Saturdays before she approached her dad again. He resisted, but Brianna knew her father's construction skills would help.

"OK, Brianna. But just once."

Brianna's dad went. It changed his life. As a builder he had focused his life on constructing custom homes. He was successful at it. Now, someone needed him to give. He got excited about the same things his daughter did. He saw the value of what World Impact was doing. He enjoyed working beside his daughter.

Brianna's dad liked it so much that he offered to manage the construction of new residences for the staff. He took a leave of absence from his company for six months to complete the project. It cost him thousands of dollars. But he received a treasure: Brianna became a compassionate activist instead of a conspicuous consumer. We build into our children motivation when we create opportunities to serve together.

Again, when we parents model right behavior, we teach lessons much more strongly than by words alone. And when we join our children in serving others, we will motivate them to care for others.

10. Play Together.

Motivation comes from relationship. It's not simply an individual endeavor. When we play together we can inspire each other to try new things. To explore new frontiers. To sample unknown foods . . .

Yes, trying something new with your children can be dangerous, but in playing together you give them the emotional support to be more adventurous. They are more apt to go out on the tightrope if they have the safety net of relationships.

Furthermore, when parents and children relax, laugh, and enjoy each other, it builds a bond between them. It creates a sense of belonging. It makes one feel whole. We build relationships by sharing fun times. If this wasn't so, then why would we ever socialize with people from work? We just worked with them for eight hours! But working together doesn't build relationships the same way that playing together does. Simply put, having fun together can motivate us.

Yes, having fun is a great way to motivate yourself and your children. The relaxed parent has discovered how to motivate his children.

FOR THE RELAXED PARENT

1. From your own experiences, give some examples that confirm "what used to motivate kids doesn't work today."
2. How does stress relate to motivation?
3. Do you agree that stressed parents see their kids as symbols? Has that attitude ever crept into your thoughts about your own kids?
4. What do you think about the author's idea to write letters to his daughter? Would this be an effective strategy for you in passing on values?
5. Which of the "Ten Tips for Motivating Your Child" seem to be the most relevant to your situation?

Skill Builder

HIGH PERFORMANCE TUNE-UP

Explain to your child that motivation is something that comes from within. It's like having a turbo-charged race engine in your car. With motivation you can go places fast! Take your child to the races—car, boat, jet ski, motorcycle, anything that has an engine. Explain how inner motivation is like a racing motor. Choose one or two of the Ten Tips for Motivating Your Child and try to apply them the same week as going to the races.

$\mathcal{P}$ARENTING $\mathcal{P}$RINCIPLE

The relaxed parent turns over areas of response-ability to his children to help them learn from the consequences.

$\mathcal{T}$WELVE

TEACHING
RESPONSE-ABILITY

———— $\mathcal{I}$f you don't knock it off, I'll stop this car and you will get out!" threatened the frustrated mother. She had been driving for nearly an hour, looking for the right beach to take her kids to.

"No, you won't," answered her four-year-old daughter; "you'll just get mad, yell at me, and say 'get out,' but you won't make me. You'll just open the door, close the door, and we'll keep driving."

Little Jackie had called her bluff. She knew how her mother would respond. The four-year-old gambled and won that particular showdown.

Perplexed, the mom kept driving, wondering how a four-year-old had become such an alert student of parental behavior.

Our kids often know how we will respond. They have been studying us all their lives. Sometimes they take advantage of that knowledge, using it to gain their freedom and to push for what they want. Call it a conspiracy. Call it manipulation. Call it sneaky.

But before you get to feel like the victim, let me remind you of one fact: You did it too!

Each of us, as one-time children, tried to manipulate our parents. It's time to come out of our denial and admit it. We would rather train our parents than have them train us. This is the problem: children attempting to train parents, as we parents are attempting to train them. There is a conflict between who is the trainee and who is the trainer.

But parents are in charge. At least, we are supposed to be. We need to assume the responsibility to discipline our kids, to help them learn from their mistakes. Discipline involves letting children receive the consequences of their actions, either direct or indirect consequences of their choices. We discipline because we love our children. We also discipline because we want them to learn right behavior, a key goal of relaxed parents. And discipline creates what I call response-ability in our children—the ability to respond properly to life situations.

Discipline is a controversial topic these days. Some folks feel we should be permissive and "let children discover for themselves their own boundaries, limits, and values."

Others feel parents should "whip the little brats into shape. Don't tolerate any challenging of the rules."

I'm somewhere in the middle. I'm afraid of both extremes. The permissive types scare me. I'm afraid their children may get run over while they are playing on the freeway of life. To put it bluntly, some of the experimental behavior that kids get into is life-threatening. Especially teens who are sexually active or misusing drugs or alcohol. In our desire to give them freedom and self-expression, they may be robbed of life.

I'm also afraid of the "keep-the-rules parents." I've seen many parents who focus on punishment. They become preoccupied with the behavior of their children. They forget that their children are people with emotions and thoughts. As a result, the kids follow the maxim "Rules without relationship lead to rebellion."

DISCIPLINE, STRESS, AND BEING PERMISSIVE

Earlier we mentioned the role of consequences in discipline. But discipline also involves stress, though the purpose is noble: Discipline *is the deliberate creation of stress in your relationship with your child for the purpose of helping him or her grow and learn.*

If you don't want stress in your life, then don't discipline.

Maybe that is why some busy parents choose the permissive approach. They just don't have the time or energy to handle the stress of discipline. But like that mechanic on the TV commercial says, "You can pay me now, or you can pay me later."

Hurried parents who resort to permissiveness aren't relaxed parents. They are worried. Sooner or later, the permissiveness catches up. The neglect and avoidance will take its toll. The bill comes due.

The relaxed parent is willing to discipline her child. Knowing that the purpose is to help her child grow and learn, she is willing to endure the extra stress that will come into her life as a result of her commitment to discipline.

Rules-oriented parents can benefit from this definition, too. Discipline focuses on learning and growing. In contrast, punishment focuses on behavior and rule keeping. Discipline helps children learn self-control. Punishment only works if there is an enforcer around.

And response-ability, which lets your child respond correctly to difficult situations, increases through discipline. We prepare our kids for life when we discipline them.

USING THE "R" WORD

That's the goal—to prepare our kids for life. How do we do it?

Well, it has to do with the "R" word. I have noticed that many teens aren't offended when they hear swearing. They are desensitized to it. They hear it all day at school from other students. The movies are full of profanities. But bring up the "R" word, and they will grimace. It is truly offensive. The word, of course, is *responsibility*.

The Classic Definition of Responsibility

I have actually observed teenagers scowl and cover their ears when they hear this offensive word. It seems the equal to a swear word.

The reason may be that we parents have overused the word, and it has lost its meaning. *Responsibility* may sound like a slogan instead if an important idea. Overfamiliar ideas begin to look like labels; their significance is lost. In fact, I think *responsibility* is a word with a P.R. problem. We parents overuse it and teenagers misunderstand it. But it is a great concept, one your teen can readily accept, once he knows its true meaning. Here's a classic definition of the word: *Responsibility is being willing to be held accountable for your behavior.*

Most teens would agree with that definition—everyone should be accountable for what he does. Though this is not a bad definition, teens will find it boring. Teens are always asking, "What's in it for me?"

The classic definition for responsibility doesn't address this question of what benefits come from being responsible. As a result, it doesn't provide motivation for the child. The picture is someone spying on the teen to make sure he does what he was supposed to do. Not very motivating, is it?

A Fresh Definition

But put another spin on the word—one that includes positive motivation—and it has a whole new ring to it. Consider this fresh definition: *Response-ability is being prepared to take on life's situations.*

Feel the motivation? Hear the excitement? Capture the movement?

This definition creates anticipation. It looks to the future. The classic definition looks to the past, "Did you do what you were supposed to do?" The new definition imagines a hopeful future where the child is prepared to take on whatever life hands him. One contains a warning—and warnings are necessary at times—but the other contains a promise—you're getting ready to become an adult.

Remember that earlier I indicated that response-ability is the ability of our children to respond to life situations as they grow into adults. That's truly what response-ability means, and children will respond to the invitation to become adults.

Talking with Your Child About the "R" Word

The best way to help your child change his thinking about responsibility from a negative to a positive—to turn *responsibility* into *response-ability*—is to have a conversation with him about the word. In your conversation, tell him of your desire to be a better parent. Treat him as a growing, changing individual by inviting his input on areas of response-ability. The conversation can begin when your child is twelve or sixteen, whenever he (or she) is ready. Depending on your own son (or daughter), the conversation may proceed something like this:

"Junior, I want to become the relaxed parent. I want to help you do more so I can do less. I want to work myself out of a job—the job of always telling you what to do and how to behave. I want to help you become more independent. My goal is to prepare you to take on life's situations."

"Huh? Whadya say, Dad?"

"I said, I'd like to help you do more so I can do less. Less telling. Less nagging."

"Seriously? Cool! . . . Hey, is this a joke?"

"No, I'm serious. I want you to be ready to take on life. Are you interested?"

"Yeah. Sure. What does it involve?"

"Let me ask you a few questions, and you give me an honest answer."

"OK, shoot."

"What do I do that makes you feel like an adult?"

"Umm. When you trust me with your new truck for Friday nights."

"OK. What do I do that makes you feel like a child?"

"When you lecture me in front of my friends."

"All right. What is one area where you could use less direction from me?"

"Hmmm. Let me see . . . Oh, I know, I could use less direction from you about my homework. I'm doing fine. Getting good grades, mostly A's and B's. I can handle it."

"I see. How about an area you could use more input or direction from me?"

"Dad, I'm worried about college. I have no idea which one. I have no clue on a major. I don't know if I'm supposed to pay for it or what? I could use your help."

"Sure, Son, let's talk about it this weekend. We can even schedule a trip to visit some colleges this semester."

"That would be great, Dad!"

"OK, Son, one last question: Are you interested in learning how to take on life's situations? Can I coach you to prepare for some situations I think you will encounter?"

"Yeah, sure, Dad."

"Great. Let's redefine a word. Let's make it our definition: Response-ability is being prepared to take on life's situations. What do you think, Son?"

"Sounds interesting. Can we get back to the part where you do less nagging and I get more freedom?"

The relaxed parent has discovered ways to help his child become prepared to take on life's situations. He understands the concept of response-ability.

USING CONSEQUENCES

One way we can help prepare our children for life is to teach them by using consequences. In a way, it is a life simulation.

I had just introduced this concept to a group of parents.

One father asked, "What is the difference between discipline and punishment? It seems to me that consequences are punishment."

"Let's say you decide that you don't want to work tomorrow, or the next day. If you kept that up, would they pay you for not working?" I asked.

"No, of course not."

"Is it punishment?"

"No. It's reality."

"That is what we are after. We want to prepare our kids for the real world. Punishment would be if you got fired for intentionally driving over your boss."

"OK, now I see it."

Consequences are different from rules. Rules are initiated by parents and enforced by parents. Consequences are tools to teach children how to be responsible for their behavior. Consequences help children make good decisions for their lives. Consequences are tools, not rules.

Keeping Our Children Accountable

Using consequences for your children's behavior will hold them accountable. Let them know in advance what those consequences will be. If you have teenagers, include them in developing specific consequences for their specific behavior. But do this in advance of needing it. Don't wait until you have a problem to think up a consequence. Anticipate which consequences you will need and discuss these with your child.

For instance, what should you do if your child forgets to pick up his or her dirty clothes? You have several options. As a parent, you can: (1) leave them there and ask your child to pick them up; (2) throw them under your child's bed; (3) pick them up; (4) throw them in the trash; (5) another option of your choice.

We discussed this situation with our parents' group. One single mom suggested her consequence.

"I got so tired nagging my daughter to pick up her junk. She was leaving her stuff all over the living room, family room, and kitchen. I work all day, so I don't have energy to come home and clean up. Something had to be done."

"What did you do?"

"I got a cardboard box and wrote 'Saturday' on the side of it. It is my 'Saturday Box.' I told my daughter Missy that if she leaves her stuff out, in the common area, it goes in the Saturday Box and she can get it out on Saturday. My exception is school books. Everything else, she'll just have to live without."

"How is it working?"

"Beautifully. You should see our house none of her stuff is trashing it like it used to."

"What about her room?" asked a mother.

"Well, that's another story. It's a mess. But I just shut the door. You know, 'choose your battles.' "

Every relaxed parent has her own strategies. The important thing is to choose those consequences, inform your children, and then stick to them. Some consequences are natural outcomes.

When a child doesn't tighten his shoestrings, eventually the shoe wobbles or even comes off as he walks to school. A child has too many fries and she can't finish her shake. (Most kids learn early to change their food order to avoid this one.)

But some natural consequences are too severe to be good teachers. When our children were little we smacked their hands if they got near something hot. We didn't say, "If you touch that barbecue, you will just have to suffer the consequences." We want to protect our kids from the full impact of natural consequences. We didn't say, "If you play out in the street, you'll get run over." We said, "Don't play in the street!"

Effective Logical Consequences

In addition, some natural consequences are not immediate enough for the child to learn to be responsible. That is when we need logical consequences. To be effective, logical consequences must seem logical to the child. They must make sense and seem appropriate. Logical consequences need to be reasonably connected to the misbehavior.

For example, a natural consequence of your child living in a messy room would be for it to become messier and for dust and mold to accumulate. The room might eventually be designated a disaster area. This is the natural course for kids with messy rooms. But the cost is too great to let the only consequence be a natural one, and the child's behavior may change only temporarily, to help him find what he needs. A logical consequence attempts to teach the lesson sooner, before the situation gets out of hand.

What do you think would be a logical consequence for a child with a messy room? Consider what one mom and author suggests.

We wrote a rule that said, "Every morning before school, your bed must be made and all towels picked up and hung in the bathroom." As a consequence of not doing this, I charge Heather $1.00 for an unmade bed and 75 cents per wet towel. During the week, I let everything else go. And I shut her bedroom door. However,

TEACHING RESPONSE-ABILITY

173

every Saturday I required Heather to clean her room. Because her idea of "clean" was different than mine, I developed a list of tasks to complete. Then after Heather cleaned, I checked the list to decide if the room looked satisfactory.[1]

Consider the consequences for a child who is smoking cigarettes. The natural consequence could be health problems, and you could warn your child about the definite correlation between smoking and lung cancer. But waiting on those consequences is too costly—it's potentially deadly—and it's not immediate. A logical consequence might work better. Here's just one suggested series of logical consequences

At first offense you might charge them the price of a pack of cigarettes each time they smoke. Since cigarettes are expensive, this can really add up. The money comes from their allowance, their earnings from work, or from earnings they receive from work done around the house. On the second offense, have the smoker research and write a report on "The Dangers of Smoking." Require it to be three pages typed and to have at least one picture or graph as a visual aid.

The third offense requires a more drastic consequence. Remember, the teen should help you in developing these consequences in advance, thus being aware of them and having ownership in them. The third offense could be that the smoker interview people with emphysema or lung cancer. He could use a tape recorder. The goal is to understand how these people have their lives shortened due to smoking.

CHOOSING OUR BATTLES

Remember, our goal is to prepare our kids to take on life's situations. We want them to be response-able. Sometimes this will involve discipline—the deliberate creation of stress in your relationship with your child for the purpose of helping him or her grow and learn.

But not too much stress. We need to choose our battles wisely, or we will be battling all the time.

At my parenting seminars, I distribute a worksheet entitled "Choosing Your Battles." It lists twenty areas of potential conflict. Parents are instructed to prioritize the issues. They are issues like chores, clean room, choice of friends, honesty, etc.

"List which of these is VIP—Very Important, Important, and Less Important. The Less Important ones are the areas you will entrust to your child. Take five minutes and prioritize."

After they complete the exercise, I shift our focus and begin a discussion about their job. "Imagine going to work tomorrow and your boss calls you into his office and says, 'We've been studying your performance review. We'd like to see some immediate improvement if you expect to continue working here.'

"You are numb with disbelief. The words are bouncing off the walls. The shock causes your head to spin.

"Your boss continues, 'We have listed eight areas we need to see marked improvement in the next month for your continued employment.'

"How would you feel? What would you like to say (or do) to your boss?"

I asked parents to imagine this scenario.

One father angrily exclaimed, "I'd let the @#!%&*$! have it! That's totally impossible!"

"I'd file a grievance with the union," said one mother.

"I would prepare a file and hire a lawyer for a wrongful termination suit," said a father.

I asked, "Is it realistic to ask for improvement on eight areas in one month's time?"

"No! Totally unrealistic!" they echoed.

"OK, let's see how we did on our 'Choosing Your Battles' worksheet." I redirect. "How many of you have more than eight VIPs on your list?" I ask for a show of hands. "All right, how many of you have five or more VIPs? . . . How many have at least five Importants and at least three VIPs—totaling eight?"

I pause for effect.

"You mean to tell me you expect your child to be working on improving in eight, ten, or twelve areas all at once? I thought we agreed that was unrealistic?"

They have been set up. Some parents smile. Some get angry. Others are confused.

"When we expect our children to improve on all fronts, we are exasperating them. We knock the wind right out of them. We steal their motivation when we are too demanding. The same way we feel when we have a demanding and unrealistic boss is the way they feel when we expect improvement in eight areas in one month."

I noticed the parents who had the most issues listed as VIP. They looked the most tired. They came across as the most rattled. They appeared to me to be on the frazzled edge. They were not relaxed parents.

Sometimes we do more by doing less.

We need to choose our battles wisely. Which issues are worth dealing with now? Which ones are worth letting go? As parents, we only have so much time, energy and emotion to put into parenting. Trying to resolve all issues is fruitless. Asking for improvement on eight or more issues is unrealistic. It might even be cruel.

Our children are ready to take on some of the issues that we have been nagging them about. They are ready to experience the consequences once we release them to it. By trying to parent on all fronts, we may have kept our kids from learning. It may be time to let go of some of the issues we used to consider "Very Important." Chances are, they weren't that important to our kids.

We can spend a lot of time majoring on the minors.

I'll never forget that night in a beautiful southern California home, as members of a parents' group began to discuss consequences.

"If we don't help our kids learn self-discipline by keeping their rooms clean, they'll grow up to be slobs," warned Carol.

"I don't know why they can't just bring the plates back to the kitchen when they are done with them. I find plates with mold on them in my daughter's room. It's gross!" exclaimed Martha.

"And when we tell them to clean up their room, it all goes in the closet," said Dick. "Everything looks good as long as you don't open the closet. The other day . . ."

The new member of the group shouted from the midst, and her urgency and honesty took several of us back. "Excuse me!" the new lady exclaimed. "I just want to remind you that there are more important things than messy rooms. I came here tonight because I wanted help. My daughter is in trouble, and it's not a messy room. You need to choose your battles carefully. A messy room, or talking on the phone too long, or moldy dishes aren't that critical when your teenager is on cocaine!"

Swooosh!! The oxygen felt like it was sucked out of the room. We were accosted by her revelation. In a flash, we had a much clearer perspective. The newcomer was right. Some things aren't that critical. Let some go so you have time to deal with the truly important issues. *Don't get sidetracked by the minor issues.*

This new voice reminded us of a corollary of Parenting Principle 11: *Choose your battles wisely, or you will be battling all the time.* While we are to turn over areas of response-ability to our children, when we get in a conflict, we must be careful. Not all battles are worth the effort, but many are. Choose carefully.

I'm so glad the newcomer spoke up. She reminded us that consequences aren't doled out for punishment, revenge, or control. Consequences are given to help our children grow into mature adults, to make the right decisions. Remember, response-ability is being prepared to tackle life situations. Help your children with this and you will help them to learn and mature.

Reflections

FOR THE RELAXED PARENT

1. Describe a time when your child demonstrated that he had been "studying" you (in order to influence you).
2. Do you see yourself more as a permissive parent or a keep-the-rules parent? Why?
3. What do you think about the fresh definition for "response-ability"?
4. How are consequences different from rules?
5. How would applying the "Choosing Your Battles" corollary help you to become more of a relaxed parent?

Skill Builder

CHOOSING YOUR BATTLES

Make a list of the issues of responsibility you are seeking to develop with your child. Prioritize them. Choose three to focus 80 percent of your parenting on. Choose three as your secondary issues. Then choose the next lower level. Delegate 1–3 to your child, saying, "This is now your responsibility. I'm not going to nag you on this. It's yours. You'll experience the consequences based on what you do."

PARENTING PRINCIPLE

*The relaxed parent guides his children
by moving from a position of control
to a position of influence.*

THIRTEEN

REMOTE-CONTROL PARENTING

*W*hat would life be like if we had remote controls for our children? We could recline in our loungers and push buttons. And we would have a keypad that really works:

Mute—The kids go silent.
Change—We can change the topic of conversation.
Pause—"Don't bother me with that now. I'll deal with it later."
Sleep—Either they, or we, would instantly slumber.
Power—We could turn them off and put them away.
Play—We immediately enjoy laughter and play together.
Menu—The kids cheerfully prepare our favorite meal and serve us.

The above-described remote control is purely imaginary, of course. *So what's the meaning of a chapter title like "Remote-Control Parenting,"* you're probably wondering right now. *Is he telling me parents can control their children from afar, that we can get our kids to be passive and compliant, doing as we command?* No, I can assure you with two daughters of my own that I do not practice nor recommend passive parenting. Remote-control parenting uses consequences to control and rechannel your children's misbehavior. When properly used, it's like parenting by remote control; in fact, it's a key way to become the relaxed parent in the area of control. And ultimately it can lead you from mere control to influencing your children's behavior, another principle of relaxed parenting.

We really need the remote control for our children. Otherwise they can control us. Our children know us well; they know what buttons to push, even how to manipulate us. That's why we need a remote control. *We* should be pushing the buttons.

Before I explain how to operate your remote control, let me demonstrate how adept our children are at control and manipulation. Let's take my teenage daughter, Nicole, as an example. She went to a sleep-over at the home of her friend, Kristi. It was for her volleyball team, ten energetic fifteen-year-old girls.

I dropped Nicole off and met Kristi's parents. They seemed normal, with a large, well-decorated home. Somehow, though, they said yes to this sleep-over in their nice home. When I left I thought, *Their house is nice, even beautiful. So why do they risk destroying it in a hormone hurricane?*

Earlier, when I was driving Nicole to Kristi's home, I thought I had this sleep-over figured out. After all, they're all pretty much the same. The girls would stay up to 1:00 or 2:00 A.M. (even though wake-up for the tournament would be about five o'clock). They would tell stories, describe boys—probably call boys. They'd make comments about the other teams' uniforms, comments about the other teams' abilities, comments about the other teams' backsides. There was much to do before hitting the sack.

But I didn't have it all figured out. Like the requirement that each girl bring one hyperactive-inducing over-the-counter candy like Snickers, M&Ms, Skittles, and other such fun snacks. And money for pizza.

Finally, enroute to the sleep-over, Nicole told me about the must-brings. It was the classic Teen Trick.

"Oh yeah, Dad. We are supposed to bring treats, sodas, and $5 for pizza."

Of course, we were already twenty minutes late. This illustrates a common teenage ploy: "Last minute urgent requests." For instance:

"Oh yeah, Mom. I almost forgot; can we swing into the Urgent Care? I promised that you would give a pint of blood."

"Hey, Dad, can you pick me up a few things on your way back from the hardware store? Just a few essentials—foundation, moisturizer, eyeliner, nail polish, nail file, panty hose, and a Raspberry Diet Ice Tea Snapple, decaffeinated? Oh, and I need it in fifteen minutes. I'm going to the movies with Shannon."

This strategy usually works. That is why they use it. The Last Minute Urgent Request is presented with intense urgency. "You must act now!" is the message. If we don't act quickly, we will be accused of not caring enough about them.

Having begun with the Urgent Request, Nicole now added the Fear and Shame tactic: "I guess I could go to the sleep-over without my treats. I'll just borrow someone else's. Maybe I could beg a few peanuts off of Kristi? I'll just drink water from the tap. I wonder what the girls will think?"

Of course, this kicks in the shame and the fear of comparison for the parent. The message is: "What kind of cheapskate parent would not buy his own flesh and blood snacks for the sleep-over?"

It's a cheap shot, but it works.

The reason we have difficulty in controlling our kids is they are too busy controlling us. They have more time and energy to strategize. Their rewards for manipulation are freedom, control, and cash, incentives that have proven themselves with humans over the centuries.

But here's the point: *Families should be run by parents, not children.* That's not the parenting principle for this chapter, but it is a truism every parent must live by. Otherwise he or she can never be the relaxed parent.

But being in charge can be especially difficult with teenagers, who begin to treat rules and even help from parents as suspect. Psychologist and counselor Haim Ginott describes the dilemma: "Parents of teenagers face a difficult dilemma: how to help when help is resented, how to guide when guidance is rejected, how to communicate when attention is taken as attack."[1]

Trying to show care may be interpreted as interfering. Trying to understand is considered prying. Helping teens make good decisions may be judged as controlling. Sometimes it seems like a no-win situation.

But the fact is, the parent is the authority in the home. And you hold the control buttons in your hand. Far from being passive, you are involved.

I'm not talking about the parent becoming a dictator. I'm saying the parent has the right to exercise her or his authority as a parent. We are responsible to help prepare our kids for life. We do this by gradually giving them more freedom and response-ability. This isn't cruel—it's loving. We have control so that we can release control, gradually, to prepare our children for real life.

In my experience, I have found the following quote by the master teacher Jesus to be true: "Whoever can be trusted with very little can also be trusted with much, and whoever is dishonest with very little will also be dishonest with much. . . . If you have not been trustworthy with someone else's property, who will give you property of your own?"[2]

Why should we give our kids a car if they haven't been responsible with a bike? Why should they get to roam the city if we can't trust them down the street? More freedom is earned as children prove they can handle it. This is the principle of progressive freedom.

We must be careful or we will find ourselves treating our children as nearly our equals. Indeed, Gosman notes that many parents let "the children set the rules for the entire household." He describes the following scene in many homes:

> Young people are consulted about everything. Should we go to Grandma's today? Can we go shopping for clothes on Saturday? The kids' schedule is what we work around, not vice versa. They can't miss a soccer game, but we can miss work or an appointment with a friend to drive them.[3]

"Homes are not meant to be democracies," Gosman concludes. He is right. Parents are in charge. Discipline is our responsibility. Kids will respect parents who decide to make order out of chaos. When we set the boundaries and stick to them, it gives our children a sense of security. We demonstrate our love for our kids when we say no.

When we discipline effectively, our children will feel loved and cared for. But don't expect them to admit this! Few kids will say, "Thanks, Dad, for restricting me from MTV for a week. I know this will really build character within me." But that's OK. The temptation's removed to veg out on trash TV like his friends. Over time, he will appreciate it.

USING THE REMOTE CONTROL

Before you can use the remote control, you must find it. Do you have this problem in your house? We do. Remote controls are forever being lost. Sofa pillows, thick chair legs, and the kids' rooms usually are playing hide-and-seek with the control. For you, maybe the dog took it to his favorite secluded spot. It's tough to find the remote control.

Finding the remote control also applies to parenting. Finding the remote control in parenting means to *define your expectations*. Defining your expectations is the first of six steps in using your parenting remote control. Let's look at each step to getting maximum use out of your parenting remote control.

1. Define Your Expectations

This is the first step to remote-control parenting. Before you can use the television remote, you need to find it. Before you can use the parenting remote, you have to "find" what you want out of your kid. You need to define what behavior you would like to see.

This may seem very obvious to some, but it is a critical first step. Can you describe the behavior you want to see in your child? Have you discovered and described your expectations in writing? I recommend putting those expectations in writing, for your children to see.

2. Inform Your Children of the Consequences

Step two is to *inform you ild of the consequences of mis-behavior*. This echoes back to n   l and logical consequences in chapter 7. What we need to do is say, "If you do this . . . this will happen. It's your choice."

In my discussions with parents, I have discovered that many tell their children what the rules are, but they don't describe the negative consequences if they disobey the rules. We might lecture them about the morality of their disobedience. We might analyze them with our psychological perspective. We may even play the victim. But we don't tell them in advance the outcome of their disobeying.

Children need to know in advance the consequences of their misbehavior. We need to be as specific as possible.

I was counseling a mother who was complaining about her eleven-year-old's room.

"It's a disaster area," said Linda (not her real name). "Dirty clothes, leftover food and plates with mold on them, wet towels on the bed, and school projects strewn everywhere!"

"A clean room is very important to you."

"Yes, it is. Very important."

"How is she responding to your nagging?" I asked.

"That's why I'm here. She's not, and I'm frustrated."

"Then she won," I said.

"What?"

"Sounds like she is in a power struggle with you over her room, and she's winning."

"With her, everything is a power struggle."

"Does it have to be?"

"That's the way it is," Linda said with weary exasperation.

"Choose your battles wisely or you will be battling all the time."

"Hmmm."

"Is a dirty room worth losing your relationship with your daughter?"

"Right now I'm so frustrated I want to ship her off to boarding school!"

"Is it worth battling over?"

"I don't know."

"She is getting ready to enter adolescence." I observed, "You need to be selective on the things you'll deal with, what you'll let go, and what you will turn over to her domain."

We talked a bit about how her daughter felt about the mess. (Obviously it didn't bother her.) Then I began asking Linda about expectations and consequences her daughter faces at home. It was soon clear that there were few expectations and fewer consequences.

"Does your daughter do her own laundry?"

"No, I do."

"Why not let her do her own laundry? She will soon realize that wet towels aren't good on her bed. She will also have to pick up her clothes and place them in her hamper and then wash them. Does she have her own hamper?"

"No."

"On your way home, buy a plastic laundry basket and tell your daughter it is hers now. She will need to put all her dirty clothes and towels in it and be responsible to wash her own. Show her how and don't rescue her. She will learn to do it or face the consequence of drying off with a wet towel and putting on dirty clothes."

"Wow, that sounds good. What about the food?"

3. Develop with Your Child Meaningful Consequences

"Food can be eaten in the kitchen. She doesn't need to eat it in her room. Make it an expectation and discuss with her a consequence if she takes food into her room."

That, by the way, is step three in becoming a remote-control parent. We need to involve our children in determining the consequences for their misbehavior. Then it is meaningful, and something they can live with. Linda was skeptical about letting her budding teenager choose the consequences.

"You mean ask her to help think up the consequence? I have always determined the consequence for her."

"Yes. She will hate it. Kids don't like to think about their negative consequences. They would rather live in the fantasy that they are immune from the Law of Cause and Effect. They are immortal, you know."

She smiled and asked, "What about lunch? She always complains about what I make her."

"Why are you making her lunch? She's old enough to make her own. She will stop complaining when she has to make her own. Just provide the essentials and tell her she can make her own or spend her own money to purchase a school lunch."

The mother paused; she stared at me. "Should I write these down?"

I told her that writing a list of expectations and consequences was a good idea. In fact, I suggested that she sit down with her daughter and draw three columns on a notebook paper.

"In the first column describe the value that is important to you," I said. "For instance, a clean room isn't as important as the life-skill of taking care of her clothes and laundry. The value in the first column could be called 'Responsible Ownership.' The second column describes the behavior you want to see. Be as specific as you can. The third column describes the negative consequence if she misbehaves."

"How many behaviors and consequences?"

"Just pick your top three or four. That will be enough."

"How do I use this?"

4. Put It in Writing

What Linda did was step four to remote-control parenting: *Record the consequences in writing.* Putting it in writing reminds your children of what they agreed to and assures you that both they and you live up to the agreement. I suggested to Linda that she make a copy for herself. You may want to do the same with your teen or preteen. After all, these things tend to disappear (with the remote control).

Post a copy in your child's room, perhaps on the inside of her door. When your daughter or son blows it, say, "It looks like you didn't do your chore of emptying the dishwasher. You have chosen to earn the opportunity to clean the entire kitchen, in addition to unloading the dishwasher."

If, like Linda, you find that she blows it more than once (not an uncommon occurrence), don't yell or threaten. Simply say, in a neutral and calm voice, "By your behavior you have chosen the consequence described under number three," and then walk away. No threats. No power struggles. No arguing.

5. Refer to and Enforce the Document

What you are doing is practicing step five: Refer to the written document of consequences as necessary. Enforce the consequences. If you or your child has any doubts, remind yourselves by looking at the agreement. But then enact the consequences as necessary. Remind your children that they get the consequences because *they* made the choice.

Linda took my advice, and things are going much better now. She is arguing less and enjoying parenting more. For Linda, remote control parenting worked with her thirteen-year-old messie. Although I cannot guarantee results—setbacks are likely—it will put you in charge, as a parent is supposed to be. And that control will make you a relaxed parent.

6. The Proper Stance

Step six, taking the stance of the relaxed parent, should be fun. But often this final step is a challenge. It is, though, the key to effective remote-control parenting. Your stance is important in baseball, especially when you are at bat. Your stance is important in basketball, especially when you are shooting a free throw. Your stance is not that important in bungee jumping, but it is important in parenting.

Consider your efforts to influence and direct your children. What works with children who are age nine does not work as well with children who are thirteen. Why is that? What difference does a few years make? It all has to do with stance.

What is your parenting position? With younger children we can take a position of direct and firm control.

"Don't put Play-Doh up the dog's nose, or I'll take it away from you."

We assumed responsibility for initiating punishment. We tried to control our precious child with rules and swift punishment for misbehavior. Generally, it worked. But now, as the child becomes older, threats of taking away the Play-Doh don't seem to carry the same impact. The control position doesn't work as well as our children get older.

Remote-control parenting means *moving from a position of control to a position of influence.* The proper position of the relaxed parent shifts. No longer do we use direct control. We give up the illusion that we can really control a teenager and move toward influence instead.

Here are the six steps for turning on and using your remote control with the children: (1) Find the remote control (define your expectations). (2) Inform your child of the desired behavior. (3) Develop with your child meaningful consequences for misbehavior. (4) Record it in writing. (5) Calmly refer to this written document when you need to, reminding your child that he gets the consequence because *he* made the *choice.* (6) Assume the position of the relaxed parent.

Using Logical Consequences

We can influence our preteen and teenage children by helping them learn to make good choices. We do this by predetermining logical consequences to their behavior. In the previous chapter we talked briefly about logical consequences. They are a variation of natural consequences. Natural consequences could be defined as "the natural results of inappropriate behavior." Here are some examples: "If you touch that stove you will be burned"; "If you ride your bike on the freeway, you will get run over"; and "If you spit into the wind, you may meet again."

But we can't rely on natural consequences to teach our children. As we noted earlier (page 172), sometimes they are too dangerous, or the stakes are too high. The better choice is to develop logical consequences that can serve as teachers for our children.

Using logical consequences will help you become more relaxed. It will help your child to be held accountable for his behavior. You don't have to assume 100 percent of the responsi-

Moving From Control To Influence	
Control	**Logical Consequences**
Used by an authority figure	Reflect the real world of cause & effect
Easily done in anger	Can be used without much emotion
Appropriate for controlling and directing young children	Appropriate for influencing and motivating preteens and teens
Tends to be unrelated to the misbehavior	Logically related to the misbehavior
Moral judgment by parent	Moral responsibility by child
Focused on the past	Focused on the present and future
Use restricted to home	Transferable to many other situations

bility for discipline. You are, in fact, assigning some of the responsibility for discipline to your child. With consequences, our children learn to discipline themselves with their choices. The parent doesn't have to make all the choices. This helps the child learn judgment and moral responsibility.

Logical consequences help prepare our children for life, because what they learn can be applied to other situations. A punishment approach may not work outside the home because no parent is around to enforce it.

Using consequences will help you on your journey to becoming the relaxed parent. It helps you switch from "rules to tools." You will feel more equipped and less stressed.

For instance, Mrs. Roberts and her daughter Kathy agreed to the following logical consequences regarding the time she must be home in the evenings:

> When I leave home in the evenings, I must be in by ten o'clock Sunday through Thursday. On Friday and Saturday nights, I must be back by midnight. If I'm going to be a few minutes late, I must call to notify. Consequences: If I do not call, or call but show up

more than thirty minutes late, for every minute I'm late, I have to come in two minutes earlier the next weekend night.

One night Kathy returned home at 1:00 A.M. to a concerned mom. Mrs. Roberts met her in the hall. "I see it's an hour past what we agreed on."

"Sorry, Mom. I forgot to call. There were some guys on the phone and—"

"Nevertheless, you were to be home at twelve. What is the consequence?"

"For every minute late I have to come in two minutes earlier next time."

"That's right. You made the choice to come in two hours earlier. Next time you will need to be home by 10:00 P.M. Good night."

"Good night, Mom."

Such conversations can occur without the parent criticizing or shaming the child. It can be done in a neutral tone of voice. Yelling, threats, and belittling do not have to occur. Simply ask the following:

"What was the desired behavior?" (curfew)

"What was the actual behavior?" (coming in late)

"What is the predetermined and written consequence?" (come in earlier the next time)

Using logical consequences puts you back in the driver's seat. The kid who pushes your buttons will lose his power over you. You will be able to help him do more as you do less. Less arguing. Less explaining. Less worrying.

LOGICAL CONSEQUENCES AND UNCONDITIONAL LOVE

Stephen Covey is best known for his wise book on leadership, *The Seven Habits of Highly Effective People*. But he has some prudent advice about family relationships, too: "The key to a happy family culture is how you treat the one that tests you the most."[4]

Logical consequences ensure fair treatment as well as self-control on your part. Both will help you to display unconditional love to your children. Such love—with no strings attached—is critical for the relaxed parent. With spelled-out consequences, enforced with an even voice and done from love, not anger, we parents learn many things. We learn to love our children when they are unlovely. We learn to love them when they are mean to their brother or sister and when they are disrespectful to us. We will even learn to love them when they embarrass us in public. This is when they most need our love—when they blow it. Indeed, our kids need our love the most when they deserve it the least.

It's easy to focus on "the bad kid"—the one who is always pushing our buttons or getting into trouble—and assign him the blame. But the relaxed parent won't spend her energy trying to fix blame; she spends her energy trying to fix the situation. As child expert Bruno Bettelheim has noted, "A happy family is not one in which nothing ever goes wrong; it is one in which when something does go wrong, the one who caused it or suffers from it is not blamed but is supported in his distress."[5]

There is a difference between being held accountable and being blamed. Being blamed creates a feeling of being trapped and being shamed. It is a put-down. Being held accountable creates a feeling of personal responsibility. It is not a loss of freedom, but is actually liberating. When people are held accountable, they are being reminded that they have the freedom to choose. Blaming jumps to the conclusion of judging. Being held accountable is one way we show love to our children. It is one strategy we can use to contend with the permissiveness and the indulgence we see in our culture. It takes love to hold our children accountable.

Love means empowering our kids to make their own decisions, to live with their own choices, and to grow through the consequences.

Devoting ourselves to what is of greatest and lasting importance is what being a relaxed parent is all about. We want to have the kind of impact on our kids so we don't have to worry about them when they are away from us. We want to know with confidence that they are capable and will make wise decisions. That happens when we move from control to influence in guiding our children.

Consider this old proverb:

> The father of a righteous man has great joy;
> he who has a wise son delights in him.
> May your father and mother be glad;
> may she who gave you birth rejoice![6]

The delight of any parent is to see his child make right decisions. (That's what it means to be righteous.) As we release our children into an uncertain world, what joy we can have to know that they are being wise in their choices.

Reflections

FOR THE RELAXED PARENT

1. How do you think your children would feel about the statement: "Families should be run by parents, not children"?
2. Do you think some parents are actually scared of their kids? Why?
3. Fred Gosman says, "Homes are not meant to be democracies." What is your opinion on this?
4. What are some of your expectations for your child? How have you communicated these to your child?
5. What would your child say are the consequences of misbehavior?
6. Review and discuss the six steps for remote control usage (page 188) with your spouse or another parent.
7. Compare and contrast control versus logical consequences, consulting the chart on page 189.

Skill Builder

UNDER THE INFLUENCE

Decide on two or three behaviors that you want to see change in your child. Write them down on paper. Describe them as positive behaviors, such as "feed the dog daily." Decide for each one a logical consequence for violating the behavior. Try to involve your child in developing these. Using consequences helps you switch from "rules to tools." It changes your perspective from control to influence.

$\mathcal{P}$ARENTING $\mathcal{P}$RINCIPLE

Relaxed parents guide their children with timeless principles based on universal truth, not with the latest formulas.

FOURTEEN

TEACHING YOUR CHILDREN WELL

$\mathcal{D}$o you ever ask yourself, "Why did I have kids?" You might respond: "Because we wanted a family." Or, "To protect our family name from extinction."

I thought about this second reason, but "Smith" isn't in any immediate danger of becoming extinct. Here are other reasons married couples give for having children:

"I wanted a child to be a lasting replica of myself."

"I wanted kids so they could take care of me when I am old."

"I want to give my children the things I didn't get growing up."

"Because we wanted a symbol of our love."

That last one takes the cake. Why do a husband and wife have to make a baby to have a "symbol of our love"? Wouldn't it be cheaper to buy a diamond ring? (Latest estimates put the cost of raising a child to age eighteen at $190,000.) Isn't it a symbol enough that they are married and committed to live and love in holy matrimony? You know, "in sickness and health, for richer and poorer," etc.?

Why do two reasonably alert, mature adults have to make another human to have a symbol of their love?

Actually, the answer is in your head. Somewhere deep in your cranial mass is *your* reason for having kids. And your reason is the right answer. My reason won't work for you. In fact, your parents' reason for having you may be different from the reason you had kids.

Each parent needs to ask herself or himself: "Why do we have children, and what do we want to pass on to them?"

Raising children is becoming increasingly difficult and risky. It seems no cumulative wisdom is gained—each generation repeats the mistakes the previous one made. Maybe we need to stop and ask ourselves:

"What can we learn from the previous generation?"

"What do we want to pass on?"

"What do we want to definitely *not* pass on?"

Legacies or Lunacies?

Every day we are making small deposits that will yield an inheritance that we pass on to our kids. The things we say to each other and the children, the way we behave, what we confront and what we let go—they all will influence our emotional and moral inheritance. My question for you is: What kind of inheritance are you passing on to your kids? A legacy or a lunacy?

We are too familiar with lunacies—the craziness that gets passed on from generation to generation: alcoholism, drug abuse, child abuse, compulsive behaviors, phobias, obsessions, prejudice, family secrets and lies, to name a few. We mentioned in chapter 8 the need to choose the legacy over the lunacy. I said then that we can be a transitional generation that decides to pass on a legacy rather than lunacy. As we explained, a legacy is more than a typical inheritance. It is an emotional and moral inheritance, one that affirms and guides the child who receives it.

Now, while your own answer to that question "Why have kids?" may differ from mine, we all agree we do want to pass on a solid legacy. Covey says, "What most people want is to live, to love, to learn and to leave a legacy."[1] We want our children to be whole, loving adults. Confident and productive, and at ease with the world. How do we do that?

This chapter is about strategizing. What is your strategy? What is it that you want to pass on to your child? How will you do this?

BEGIN WITH A BLESSING

Have you decided what legacy you would like to leave your children? You may want to begin by bestowing a blessing on your children. That's right, a blessing!

I once led a father-daughter weekend in which fathers affirmed their daughters and were to pass on a legacy to them by bestowing "The Blessing," a symbolic act based on a biblical rite. In our hectic culture, fathers seldom affirm their daughters as women. They seldom express their love to their daughters in a significant, symbolic way. In previous generations, and in other cultures, including ancient Israel, fathers would pass on words of encouragement and affirmation to their daughters and sons. These words of love and commitment are called "The Blessing."[2]

The word *blessing* in Hebrew literally means *to kneel*. The word picture is to show honor and humility to another.[3] To bless means to proclaim a full and significant life on another.

This may all sound confusing to you. I must confess that the concept was a bit foreign to me for some time. I began to really understand this idea when a friend from Uganda demonstrated an African custom. Placide emigrated from Uganda to southern California several years ago and was adjusting well. His mother-in-law came to visit one summer and fell seriously ill. I heard about it and decided to visit her. Another friend and I went to the hospital, and we enjoyed our visit with her. Though she still seemed weak, this woman displayed kindness and real interest in us. Later, I sent flowers and arranged for some meals to be brought to their home.

Placide's mother-in-law recovered well enough to make the trip back home to Uganda. She died a few weeks later.

Placide called and asked if he could stop by my office. "I just want to come for a few minutes."

"Sure, come on over," I agreed.

Placide arrived and asked me to sit in my chair. "I am going to offer you a Ugandan blessing. This is how we do it in Uganda when we want to say thank you. When we want to show our honor and respect. This is how we show gratitude."

He got down on his knees and placed his hands on my knees. He smiled and said:

"Thank you Tim, my brother, for all that you have done for me, and my family. You were there when we needed it. You are a faithful friend."

I looked into Placide's eyes. I could tell that he was very serious about what he was saying. It was clear that he meant every word he said. I was touched. Maybe it was having my friend, who happens to be black, call me "brother." Maybe it was his hands on my knees, conferring a blessing. Maybe it was his humble position, down on his knees. Maybe it was all of these. I'm not sure. But one thing I know; I received a blessing. I felt affirmed and valued.

Then Placide began to pray, "Father God, thank you for Tim and his compassion for me and my family. Thank you for the love he showed to Ellen and our family during this difficult time. May you give him strength, health, and prosperity. Bless him in the way he has blessed us. Amen."

I was stunned. I wasn't sure how to receive this marvelous gift. It was a very spiritual moment. Then I realized how important a blessing can be. The closest replica we have is the toast done by the best man at a wedding. For some, that may be the only blessing the newlywed couple receives.

Do we need to wait until we get married to receive the blessing? Of course not; we can design ways to pass on affirmation to our children while young. They live among a generation desperate for belonging, in a society where some of the most vital emotional needs are going unmet. We parents can be instrumental in affirming our children.

By what we say and do we can affirm their personal worth. Here are three simple things you can do to boost your child: (1) Write your child a note describing what qualities you like about her/him. (2) Ask your daughter or son to help plan a family day or vacation. (3) Keep your child's current picture at your workplace.

Here are three simple statements you can say to your child (there are many others) to make her or him feel special: (1) "I have confidence in you." (2) "Thanks for being yourself. I like being around you." (3) It sounds like you have been doing some good thinking."

Of course, the formal blessing is a special occasion, when you can honor the child in a tangible way. Mothers can do it as well as fathers, and the ways we do it are limited only by our imaginations. It usually involves touching your child (hand to shoulder, to head, or, like Placide, to knee). It often is in public, though it can be just the two of you.

After my experience with the African blessing, I determined to pass on the blessing to my children. I wanted to leave a legacy of love. I discovered that other dads did too, so we planned the father-daughter weekend.

At the father-daughter retreat, we helped dads pass on the blessing to their daughters. I presented an acrostic to help dads develop a modern blessing. It spells the word *BLESS*:

Bond physically. Too many dads back away from their girls when they need it the most. Daughters need to experience the father-love and affection that only a dad can give.

Lifelong relationship. Daughters need to know that their fathers are committed to them. They need to know that their dad wants to have a relationship with them, one that is based on commitment, not performance.

Esteem highly. Daughters often wonder if they are valued by their fathers. Dads can express their love and affirm their daughter's value.

Spoken word. Dads can speak words to their daughters that will affirm them and make them feel loved and accepted. Fathers are in a unique position to affirm their daughters as women.

Special future. Daughters often struggle with identity. A wise father can speak positive words to his daughter. "I can see you being a very competent and compassionate person," or "I know that you have a real love for animals. Maybe that will be part of your future. What do you think?"

Those are the critical components to the blessing.

Did you receive anything like this when you were a child? In most cultures, you wouldn't. In the Jewish tradition, children are affirmed and welcomed into the faith at their Bar Mitzvah (son) or Bas Mitzvah (daughter). It is an important time of celebration and affirmation.

At the father-daughter retreat, we asked dads to go on a walk and pass on these five points of the blessing to their daughter. We suggested creative and symbolic activities to illustrate each point.

FOOTPRINTS

At our retreat Bruce had enjoyed a wonderful afternoon with his daughter, Jen. On the beach, they had crafted a sand sculpture representing their relationship. They had enjoyed a tasty lunch at a trendy beachside cafe. Bruce affirmed his stepdaughter with the five points of BLESS. As they walked back to the hotel, they were deep in conversation. The parking lot they were walking through had recently been oiled. They didn't notice it until they began walking on the next lot which had not been treated. They saw their footprints. To their shock, they had left two sets of footprints, walking side by side, all across this large parking lot.

At first, they were embarrassed. *How could we not see that the lot was recently oiled?* they asked themselves. As they stared at the lines of four footprints tracing across the parking lot, they realized something. *This is what this weekend is all about! Leaving a mark! Making monuments of our relationship!* This insight made them feel better.

They still had to clean off their shoes; but they now have a personalized memorial of their weekend and of the blessing which was given. If they want to, they can drive to Santa Monica and visit their footprint monument!

Leaving a mark. Making a customized monument. Passing on a legacy. What are you passing on to your children? What would happen to the children in our country if they received some form of blessing from their parents? Would they feel dignity and respect? Would they feel empowered and supported?

Probably yes to all of these. I strongly encourage you to present a blessing to your children. The blessing may be marked by a one-time event, but it often comes from casual, recurring times together. Remember, the blessing will affirm and encourage your children. One result is they will receive a strong legacy of love.

PARENTING PARADIGM SHIFT

As parents, we need a paradigm shift. A paradigm is how you look at the world, a pattern for understanding and explaining certain aspects of reality. Currently, in our culture, we are caught up in the personality paradigm—what makes me look good, or what makes my child look good. To be the relaxed parent we need a paradigm shift to a character-based paradigm. We need to be more concerned about "what lies within us" and what lies within our children. Oliver Wendell Holmes said it more than a century ago: "What lies behind us and what lies before us are tiny matters compared to what lies within us."

Unfortunately, we live in a culture that is enchanted with externals. Popularity, possessions, status, and personality are the standards by which we measure ourselves. It hasn't always been this way. Holmes's words echo what was once the prevailing attitude: The inner character is more significant than outer possessions.

Our culture has shifted its focus from character to personality. "Image is everything" has become the motto for many. As parents we must evaluate our own definition for success. Do you truly believe personal character is the foundation for lasting success? Few of us doubt that qualities such as honesty, integrity, humility, courage, loyalty, and justice have more enduring and universal value than status, reputation, wealth, and position. We appreciate knowing people who display patience, simplicity, modesty, and living by the Golden Rule. But we may act it (the "image") more than we practice it.

The personality myth teaches that the goal is to be liked, so do what it takes to be liked. This obsession on externals forces us to focus on what we *do* rather than who we *are*. It makes us and our children vulnerable to the opinion of others. It often compels people to strive to earn and achieve so they will have the goods which will proclaim their worth.

Instead we need to teach our children well by focusing on our—and their—inner qualities. We need to help develop their character.

Child expert Wes Haystead says such character starts and ends with the parent: "The parent will see in the child a reflection of what the child has seen in the parent."[4] Concerning character and children, motivational speaker Zig Ziglar adds:

> Regardless of the direction our children choose to go, they are going to need a solid moral, practical, ethical, common-sense foundation from which they can launch their careers. Dr. Robert Coles of Harvard, after a twenty-year study, concluded that parents who want to give their children the best chance for success in life will teach them strong moral values.
>
> When we start with character as a base, our options are virtually limitless.[5]

MOVING FROM FORMULAS TO PRINCIPLES

Limitless options. That is a wonderful inheritance to pass on to your children. It begins with character. It begins with helping our children build their lives around proven, timeless principles. Covey argues, correctly I believe, that character "is based on the fundamental idea that there are *principles* that govern human effectiveness—natural laws in the human dimension that are just as real, just as unchanging and arguably 'there' as laws such as gravity are in the physical dimension."[6]

The relaxed parent is committed to discovering these principles. She doesn't put much faith in formulas. Formulas aren't always transferable. Because a formula works remarkably well with one child doesn't mean it will work well with all children. The relaxed parent has shifted her study from formulas to principles. Formulas are culturally, demographically, or situationally specific. In other words, formulas may work in Bakersfield, but they may fail in Boston. They may work in one family, but not the family next door.

Principles are distinct from formulas. Principles for parenting differ from formulas because they are proven, fundamental truths that have universal application. Principles are transferable from situation to situation, from family to family.

If a parenting principle is true, it will be effective in Bakersfield *and* Boston. When principles are integrated into a parent's thinking, they begin to shape his or her character. In time, the character-shaping produces a habit based on principles. Effective habits are behaviors that are desirable and based on principles.[7]

Our goal, then, is to search for principles based on timeless truths and apply these to our parenting. Where do we find timeless and universal truths? Probably not in the self-help section at your local bookstore.

I decided to do a little research at Borders Bookstore, one of those new super bookstores in town. I made my way past the cappuccino bar, overstuffed chairs, videos, compact discs, listening stations, and live entertainment on to the books, about 180,000 of them. I bought a double latté and browsed the self-help and parenting sections. I was pleased to discover my book to my daughter, *Letters to Nicole*, and other fine literary works.

But I could see trouble brewing. The books didn't agree. The trendy psychological books conflicted with the values-based books. The liberals challenged the conservatives. The conservatives blamed the liberals. What was important to one camp was irrelevant to another. I could hear the authors of the various tomes challenging each other to battle.

Consider the output in our culture. Are you happy with what you see happening among our children and youth? I didn't think so.

I believe the results today derive from the trendy parenting fads of the past thirty years. The advice has been both trendy (changing over time) and contradictory. One year a parenting authority will say, "We need to let children express themselves in a value-free environment." The next year, another authority will declare, "We need to provide specific guidelines and a strict moral code for our children." They can't both be right—they contradict each other. We live in a pluralistic society, but the advice on parenting *can't all be right*. Somebody has to be wrong. I know this isn't politically correct, so let me rephrase that last sentence: "Somebody has to be reality-challenged."

A CALL FOR PRINCIPLE-CENTERED PARENTING

I think it's time for principle-centered parenting. There are *three necessary components for principle-centered parenting*: (1) proven, timeless principles, (2) a long-term paradigm, and (3) proof that these work.

Where do we find these proven, timeless principles for parenting? I believe the most reliable source is not the latest top-selling parenting book on *The New York Times* Best-sellers List. Let's ignore the trendy, faddish books promoting this year's rage on parenting. Instead, I'm endorsing the best-selling book of all time—the Bible. I believe that we can discover useful and reliable principles in Scripture. Why? Because the Bible has been tested and used with satisfaction for centuries, or it wouldn't be read or purchased by millions.

Notice how that book meets the criteria of components two and three of our principle-centered parenting. In the Bible we discover a long-term paradigm, one that views parenting from a broader perspective. A perspective that looks at the impact generations have on generations. We also discover that each person is held accountable for individual decisions; personal responsibility and consequences for choices are emphasized.

Principles need to be transferable, that is, they need to work in different cultures and situations. In the Old and New Testaments we encounter principles that are as relevant today as they were three thousand years ago. If they are proven with time and experience, and if they have been tested by a variety of cultures and generations, they are worth our attention.

For instance, let's consider one of the Ten Commandments. The fifth one reads, "Honor your father and your mother, so that you may live long in the land the Lord your God is giving you."[8] In every culture, in every generation, it is critical that children honor and obey their parents. If they didn't, it could be disastrous.

"Honey, don't go outside the cave, there could be a Tyrannosaurus roaming about."

"Nah-nah-nah-nah-nah-nah! I don't have to. There is no rule that makes you the boss. I can do want I want." Bratty child runs outside.

"Arrumphh!" Gulp. "Ahhh!" Dinosaur eats small child. End of generation.

Obeying your parents is good for you. It is a timeless principle.

Principle-centered parenting believes that there are certain universal values, values that are admirable in all cultures, for all time. Principle-centered parenting affirms the existence of absolutes: universal laws that govern relationships like natural laws govern nature.

Consider what Denis Waitley, the motivational speaker and author, argues:

> The youth culture with its characteristic epidemics is merely a reflection of the new bankruptcy in morality and inner values. If there are no moral absolutes, if morality depends on the situation and circumstance, if people do what "feels good," ultimately they will lose their integrity and self-respect, and eventually this will lead to personal hopelessness and social chaos. When self-respect is lacking, people have a long list of "wants." They want love without commitment. They want benefits and perks without working for them; they want satisfaction without responsibility. . . . Children learn to be more concerned with their rights than their responsibilities. Rights without responsibilities are euphemistically called entitlements.[9]

We need a moral compass for ourselves and our children. The loss of absolutes within our culture has left us with uncertainty and a wimpy relativism. We really aren't sure. We need to discover, or rediscover, truths we can count on. Values we can believe in. Principles we can model in front of our children. The alternative is to continue what we are doing, and somehow keep ourselves busy so we don't notice that our kids are growing up with an acute sense of entitlement, and a dull sense of responsibility.

Use some source book as a standard. I heartily recommend the Bible. Whatever your choice, your child will benefit from a standardized, reliable moral compass to point the way.

ADAPTING PRINCIPLES TO INDIVIDUAL CHILDREN

Have you ever asked yourself, *Why do "bad" kids come from good families?* I believe it is mainly due to the use of rigid formulas. Formula-based parents typically discover an approach which works great for the first child and continue to use it; then the formula "blows up" on the second. Formula-oriented parents try to make their kid fit into their prescription.

A strong-willed child senses this and thinks, *I can really tweak their beak and win the power play here. I simply need to mess up their formula. I need to show them that just because it worked on the first child, it won't work on me!*

The principle-based parent knows that the principle will take some customizing for each child. The parent won't always use the same approach, though he keeps the same principle. The parent recognizes the goal is to shape the character of the child, not simply his outward behavior. The principle-oriented parent understands the "Eddie Haskell Factor." You may remember Eddie as the two-faced friend of Wally Cleaver in "Leave It to Beaver." He always tried to "butter up" Wally's dad and look good. With the Eddie Haskell Factor, a child may seem very polite and courteous to a parent but is actually a conniving, self-centered hoodlum internally. The principle-oriented parent responds to the "Eddie Haskell Factor by focusing on the child's character instead of his behavior.

By the way, children bent on challenging parents have a more difficult time with principles than formulas. Formulas are easy to disprove. Principles are more difficult to challenge because they have been standing for centuries. Formulas focus on what the parents do. The majority of the action is their responsibility. Principles focus more on what the child learns. The majority of the responsibility is the child's.

Principle-oriented parenting gives parents a North Star for navigating child-rearing waters. It gives them direction as they adjust to the individual differences of each child. It helps parents focus on the issues that are truly important, not simply obnoxiously urgent. These are the issues of character, who they are becoming from the inside out.

Reflections

FOR THE RELAXED PARENT

1. What prompted you to have children—an experience, an insight, or something someone said?
2. Do you agree that ours is a transitional generation, one that can turn our inheritance from lunacy to legacy?
3. Read the five elements of the blessing listed on page 199. Did you receive anything like this when you were a child? If not, what impact do you think such an event would have had on you?
4. How does a principle-based approach to parenting help a parent to relax?
5. What are some universal and proven principles that apply to parenting? Try to list at least five.

Skill Builder

THE BIG FIVE

Reflect on some of the principles that you listed under 5 above. What would you say are the top three parenting principles? Spend time thinking about them. See if you can develop one way to apply each parenting principle to your family. For instance, if one of your parenting principles is "More freedom is given as it is responsibly earned," one of the applications might be: "Since you acted responsibly with an 11:00 P.M. curfew, you have earned a midnight curfew."

FIFTEEN

BECOMING
THE RELAXED PARENT

$\mathcal{N}$o two children ever have the same parents. As each child is born, the parents adapt and change from the people they were when the previous child was born. For one thing, Mom and Dad are older now. For another, they have certain experiences to draw from. Child and parents grow together. At least, that is what is desirable.

When our first daughter was born, people smiled and said, "Good luck trying to keep up with her."

They were right. We have been trying to keep up with our two daughters ever since. As our children enter each developmental stage of childhood and adolescence, we breathlessly try to keep the pace. New challenges, new issues, new perspectives accompany each unique stage. Being an effective parent means being a lifelong learner. Parenthood is a life of continuing growth and change. The relaxed parent learns from his children as well as being their teacher. Consider Wes Haystead's experience:

What worked with Child Number One tended to bomb royally with Child Number Two. Everything I thought I had nailed down with Child Number Two seemed to shake loose with Child Number Three. By this time in my life, with my beard graying—some would say it has long passed that stage,—my hair thinning and my waist thickening, the unique personalities of each of my children keep me from settling too easily into the torpors of middle age. From peek-a-boo to piggyback rides to puberty, from cartoons to cars to college, from diapers to dentists to drug awareness, the ever-changing child pushes the parent to stretch in ways never dreamed of before Baby Number One.[1]

Kids have a way of making us grow up.

That is what this book has attempted to do—to help prepare you for the changes and challenges of parenting. If you are prepared, you will be less stressed. In fact, you may even be relaxed! The relaxed parent grows and learns and is committed to developing closeness in his family.

FOUR MARKS OF A CLOSE FAMILY

What makes for a close family? Based on research with thousands of families,[2] the husband-wife research team of Merton and Irene Strommen found four elements of a close family:

- *Show affection.* Expressions of affection from parents are vital. Children need to know they are loved through both verbal expressions and nonverbal, physical signs. Every parent needs to find a way to express affection that is natural and comfortable for both the parent and the child.
- *Spend time together.* When parents spend time with their children, they increase the opportunity to express love and care for each other, and to have meaningful conversations.
- *Build trust.* As parents and children spend time together, trust is built. Spending time *apart* can also be used to build trust and measure the amount of responsibility and freedom a child can handle without parental supervision.
- *Develop support systems.* A close and caring family is one whose members offer support to each other. It provides security and freedom. Security allows family members the freedom to expand, grow, and experiment. It also provides them with the freedom to fail as well as succeed.[3]

Having a close family requires time and work; but it is worth it. After analyzing their findings, the Strommens concluded,

Adolescents in homes characterized by love and affectionate caring are better able to resist negative behaviors and more free to develop in positive ways. For instance, there is significantly less social alienation among adolescents whose parents emphasize nurturance, as well as less involvement in drug or alcohol use and sexual activity. In nurturing homes we find more adolescents who know how to make friends and maintain good relationships with them; more who are involved in helping-type behaviors and more who tend to view religion as a liberating and challenging force in their lives.[4]

The relaxed parent works to establish closeness in the home. He doesn't wait for tomorrow. He realizes there will never be an ideal time to build a relationship. There will never be an ideal time to teach. There will never be an ideal child to learn or an ideal parent to guide the process. All we have is the reality of this day, this child, and this parent.

When we provide closeness for our child, we provide security. In a culture of hassled, hurried, and hostile people, a safe harbor is a welcome sight.

Security as provided by society is fine, but it cannot give one inner security, neither emotional warmth and well-being, nor self-respect, nor a feeling of worthwhileness. All these *only parents can give to their child,* and they can do so best when they also give them to each other. And if one fails to get them from one's parents, it is extremely difficult to acquire these feelings later in life, and they will remain shaky, at best. Thus everything depends on whether the modern family can provide this emotional security based on personal intimacy and the mutual love and respect of all its members. [Emphasis added][5]

Being relaxed comes out of personal security. The relaxed parent is secure in his (or her) role as a parent. He is content to be a parent and doesn't have to live his life through his kids. The relaxed parent is committed to building a relationship with his child as well as setting boundaries and consequences. The relaxed parent understands that a close family makes for a strong family. As the biblical proverb says,

> By wisdom a house is built,
> and through understanding it is established;
> through knowledge its rooms are filled
> with rare and beautiful treasures.[6]

What is the greatest treasure for a parent? For me, a home established on wisdom—on timeless, proven principles—that is a beautiful treasure. It is more than acquisition or success.

The road to becoming the relaxed parent is trod in small steps, not big ones. Just baby steps. Small, microsteps forward.

Don't rush it. Don't push yourself too much. Don't get stressed about your progress. After all, this is about becoming the *relaxed* parent.

To help you with your baby steps, consider the following ideas. I call them the "Fifty-Two Baby Steps Toward Becoming the Relaxed Parent." The listing includes items to say, and many things to do. Of course, with fifty-two you can choose one a week to work on. The listing is not in order of importance; all fifty-two should be equally helpful.

FIFTY-TWO BABY STEPS
TOWARD BECOMING THE RELAXED PARENT

1. Encourage your children to handle and solve their own problems as much as possible.
2. Permit your children to be responsible for every task they can physically handle.
3. Don't always protect your children from the pain of their mistakes.
4. If your children forget something, let them experience the consequences. Don't rescue. The consequences will promote greater personal responsibility in the future.
5. Choose your battles wisely, or you will be battling all the time.

6. Take your One-A-Day Vitamin. Pick one tidbit of advice you want to give your children, then swallow it. (Keep it to yourself.)
7. Exhibit self-control by not making every moment a teachable moment.
8. Spend time building your relationship with your children. Remember that rules without relationship lead to rebellion.
9. Make sure the guidelines are clear. Remember that relationship without rules leads to anarchy.
10. Set boundaries even if they are unpopular. Remember that families are not to be democracies; they are to be run by parents, not children.
11. Connect freedom with responsibility. The worst indulgence is not to make your child responsible for his behavior.
12. Parents of teens need to move from a position of control to a position of influence.
13. Don't always rescue your children from disappointments, which can help them handle failure and imperfection in the future.
14. Model your values to your children. The values we hope to see lived out by our children will most likely be values they see lived out in us.
15. Affirm character more than achievement. Affirmation of your child's character builds character. Praise for your child's achievement builds performance.
16. Our children's happiness should not be our first concern. Their growth should be. Have in mind one area in which you can help your children grow.
17. Include the child in developing the consequences. For logical consequences to work, they must seem logical to the child.
18. Meet as a family once a week to plan schedules, teach values, and show love to each other.
19. Be human enough with your kids to share your weaknesses as well as your strengths. Be honest in your relation-

ships with your children, even confessing to a mistake. We build bridges when we share from a point of weakness. We build walls when we speak from a position of strength.

20. Define one character quality you'd like to see developed in your child. Our goal should be to develop our child's character, not promote his popularity.
21. Have a weekly family fun time. Parents who have fun with their children have more energy to discipline—but don't need to.
22. Schedule a one-on-one "date" with each of your kids at least monthly.
23. Include the children in planning the family vacation, including the budget.
24. Be willing to say no to inappropriate requests. This teaches your child respect for the needs of others.
25. A long-term focus means being committed to your child's needs, not simply his wants. Say yes when you can, and no when you must.
26. Affirm your children's individuality within the context of community. Affirm how they are unique, but connect that distinctive with their contribution to the "team."

We're halfway there. (If you're doing one a week, it's early July now.) If you have adopted several of these ideas, you know your children better and you are a more relaxed parent—your children probably are more relaxed, too. Here's the second set of twenty-six steps that will help you become the relaxed parent.

27. Be sure to enforce the consequences in order not to forego necessary discipline. Discipline is the deliberate creation of stress in your relationship with your children for the purpose of helping them grow and learn. The relaxed parent is able to discipline because he isn't afraid of the added stress.
28. If your children misbehave in restaurants or grocery stores, take away a privilege. Next time, come prepared

to play a game to keep them entertained. Ask for a kid's menu. Have him hunt for certain objects in each store aisle. Remind him to behave so he won't lose his privilege like last time.

29. If your children fight over who gets to sit in the front seat, assign the seat by certain months to each child. If you have two children, alternate months.

30. To encourage reading, assign a family reading hour. Have the phone machine take calls. Make a snack to share and try to read in the same room.

31. Restrict TV watching to a certain amount each day. If your child wants more, he can earn it by reading, exercising, or doing a chore. Track with a chart posted near the TV.

32. Remind your children that you love them even when they don't live up to your expectations. After disciplining your children, sometimes a note expressing this can be helpful.

33. If your children are using the phone too much, set a daily limit and stick to it. This might be a fifteen-minute limit on all calls, no calls after 9:00 P.M. weekdays and 10:30 P.M. weekends. If they don't follow these standards, they lose their phone privileges for a week.

34. The relaxed parent has a written driving agreement with his teenager. The use of the car is a privilege, not a right. Use of the car is connected with taking care of it, driving safely, and possibly grades.

35. If your child is pushing the limits, select two or three behaviors you want to change the most. Let your child know what these are. Let him know there will be consequences for these. You are focusing on these. Don't worry about the other issues. Follow through with the promised consequence.

36. Be willing to risk temporary unpopularity with your child when you won't compromise your standards, and, instead, impose consequences.

37. Understanding the trends in childhood may help us understand our own child. Try to read one magazine or

newspaper article each week that deals with trends with
kids.

38. Each year, hand over an area of new responsibility to
your children. For example, on their birthday you could
give them the responsibility of making their lunch. The
parent doesn't have to do it anymore! Such action is part
of treating our children as family members, not guests.

39. Giving children too much may be giving them too little.
Write a plan that indicates when you plan to give each
child major gifts. For example, you may determine to
purchase her a personal stereo when she is ten years old.
This will help you not give her too much too soon.

40. Model for your child what you want to see in him. The
parent will see in the child a reflection of what the child
has seen in the parent.

41. More freedom is given as it is responsibly earned. Allow
your children a broader turf if they can handle it.

42. Model your faith in front of your child. Let her see you
pray and worship.

43. Decide together on a service project that you can do as a
family. Feed the homeless. Serve at a shelter. Take a cross-
cultural trip together.

44. Be willing to let go of your children, and encourage them
to prepare to leave home one day. Develop a countdown
to independence chart, indicating years left and corre-
sponding monuments. For example, when your son gets
his driver's license at age sixteen, mark it on the chart.

45. Include your children in your daily activities. Take them
with you when you run errands. Introduce them to other
adults. If it is appropriate, include them in the conversation. Send the message that you are proud of your child.

46. Listen to your child. Study your child to find which time
of day she likes to talk. Try to schedule your availability
to tune in to your child at that time. Eliminate distractions. Then prepare a snack and enjoy a good heart-to-
heart conversation.

47. Encourage laughter. Watch a funny sitcom. Go to a comedy club together. Listen to old Bill Cosby records from the library. Swap jokes. Rent old comedies on video.

48. Write your child. Send funny cards or serious letters. Kids love to get mail. They seldom do, so use this opportunity to pass on your love and affirmation.

49. Give your child a party. Birthdays, graduation, baptism, communion, first soccer goal scored, meet-my-new-puppy party, whatever reason! Show honor by focusing on your child and the occasion.

50. Show up at their activities. Recitals, games, plays, performances, and even practices are opportunities for you to show your love and interest.

51. Love yourself. The relaxed parent understands that parenting is draining. She models to her children that she likes herself and takes care of herself. At times this means a break from kids. The relaxed parent knows that to parent effectively she will need times of rest and exercise. This helps her keep the normal stress of parenting in check.

52. Decide on what your kid could do more of and you less of. Then initiate your plan—your plan to become the relaxed parent!

If something is worth doing, it is worth doing—even if it is done without perfection. These baby steps are worth doing, even if you don't do them well. At least you are trying! That is what baby stepping is all about. Small steps in the right direction.

To me, that is success: *small steps in the right direction.*

The relaxed parent enjoys the journey, even if it is one step at a time.

NOTES

Chapter 1: Parenting Fantasies
1. As cited in David Rice, *Parents in Control* (Eugene, Oreg.: Harvest House, 1987), 172–73.

Chapter 2: *Suave Con Estilo*
1. John K. Rosemond, "Family Counselor," *Hemispheres,* (United Airlines in-flight magazine), February1993, 81.

Chapter 3: Parenting in Reality:
1. Bill Cosby, *Fatherhood* (Garden City, N.Y.: Doubleday, 1986), 54.
2. Adele Faber and Elaine Mazlish, *Liberated Parents, Liberated Children* (New York: Avon, 1990), 223.
3. Ibid., 223–25.

Chapter 4: Hurried, Hassled and Hushed
1. As quoted in Marie Winn, *Children Without Childhood* (New York: Pantheon, 1983), 64.
2. Ibid., 65.
3. Ibid., 122.
4. Associated Press, "Kids Getting a Tough Start" (Thousand Oaks) *News Chronicle*, 29 March 1993, B6.
5. David Elkind, *All Grown Up and No Place to Go* (Reading, Mass.: Addison-Wesley, 1984), 179.

6. Neil Postman, *The Disappearance of Childhood* (New York: Delacorte, 1982), 151.

7. David Elkind, *The Hurried Child* (Reading, Mass.: Addison-Wesley, 1989), Prologue.

8. Winn, *Children Without Childhood*, 124.

9. Ibid., 127.

10. Ibid.

11. Donna Gaines, *Teenage Wasteland* (New York: Random House, 1991), 244–45.

12. Adapted from Postman, *The Disappearance of Childhood*, 80.

13. Winn, *Children Without Childhood*, 134.

14. Elkind, *All Grown Up*, 179.

Chapter 5: Princes and Princesses

1. Fred Gosman, *Spoiled Rotten* (New York: Villard, 1992), 18.

2. Ibid., 41.

3. Jean D. Okimoto and Phyllis J. Stegall, *Boomerang Kids* (Boston: Little, Brown, 1987), 12.

4. Ibid., 60.

5. Gosman, *Spoiled Rotten*, 206.

6. Lee Hausner, *Children of Paradise* (Los Angeles: Jeremy Tarcher, 1990), 214.

7. Susan Littwin, *The Postponed Generation* (New York: Morrow, 1986), 219.

8. Gosman, *Spoiled Rotten*, 51.

Chapter 6: Spoiled-Rotten Kids

1. Donna Gaines, *Teenage Wasteland* (New York: Random House, 1991), 102.

2. Ibid., 253–54.

3. Marie Winn, *Children Without Childhood* (New York: Pantheon, 1983), 127.

Chapter 7: The Forty-Year-Old Adolescent

1. The author leads more than a score of (over thirty) seminars each year, including parents' seminars. Tim Smith is available for speaking at community parenting seminars, dads' workshops, corporate luncheon

seminars, and family conferences. For a detailed brochure, write: Wordsmith; Tim Smith; P.O. Box 7736; Thousand Oaks, CA 91359–7736.
2. Charles Bradshaw, *You and Your Teen* (Elgin, Ill.:David C. Cook, 1985), 11.
3. "Young Turks," *First*, 14 February 1995, 24.
4. Ibid.
5. Andree Brooks, *Children of Fast-Track Parents* (New York: Viking, 1989), 115.

Chapter 8: From Generation to Generation
1. Tim Kimmel, *Legacy of Love* (Portland, Oreg.: Multnomah, 1989), 223–224.
2. John 8:32; *New American Standard* version.
3. H. Norman Wright, *The Power of a Parent's Words* (Ventura, Calif.: Regal, 1991), 54.

Chapter 9: The Relaxed Relationship
1. Jane Swigart, *The Myth of the Bad Mother* (New York: Doubleday, 1991), 114.
2. Frank Minirth, Brian Newman, and Paul Warren, *The Father Book* (Nashville, Tenn.: Nelson, 1992), 205.
3. H. Norman Wright, *Always Daddy's Girl* (Ventura, Calif.: Regal, 1989), 41. Wright notes that such affirmation helps our daughters to realize they are not sexual objects but important individuals.
4. Linda Eyre and Richard Eyre, *Teaching Your Children Values* (New York: Simon & Schuster, 1993), 28.

Chapter 10: The Relaxed Conversation
1. H. Norman Wright, *The Power of a Parent's Words* (Ventura, Calif.: Regal, 1991), 87.

Chapter 11: How to Motivate Your Kids
1. David Elkind, *The Hurried Child* (Reading, Mass.: Addison-Wesley, 1989), 28–29.
2. Ken Davis, *How to Live with Your Kids When You've Already Lost Your Mind* (Grand Rapids, Mich.: Zondervan, 1992), 107.
3. Ibid., 111.

4. See Andree Brooks, *Children of Fast-Track Parents* (New York: Viking, 1989), 234.

5. Davis, *How to Live with Your Kids*, 126.

Chapter 12: Teaching Response-ability

1. Teresa A. Langston, *Parenting Without Pressure* (Colorado Springs: Piñon, 1994),146–47.

Chapter 13: Remote-Control Parenting

1. Haim Ginott, *Between Parent and Teenager* (New York: Avon, 1982), 23.

2. Luke 16:10, 12; *New International Version*.

3. Fred G. Gosman, *Spoiled Rotten* (New York: Villard, 1992), 144.

4. Stephen Covey, *USA Weekend* Forum, America OnLine, 16 January 1996.

5. Bruno Bettelheim, *A Good Enough Parent* (New York: Knopf, 1987), 333.

6. Proverbs 23:24–25; NIV.

Chapter 14: Teaching Your Children Well

1. Stephen Covey, *USA Weekend* Forum, America OnLine, 16 January 1996.

2. The classic biblical example is of the patriarch Israel giving specific blessings to each of his twelve sons in Genesis 49:1–28. The concept of the blessing is discussed in great detail in the best-selling book *The Blessing*, by Gary Smalley and John Trent (Nashville, Tenn.: Nelson, 1986).

3. Laurence O. Richards, *Expositiory Dictionary of Bible Words* (Grand Rapids, Mich.: Zondervan, 1985), 130. The definition of the blessing is discussed in depth in Smalley and Trent's *The Blessing* (see previous note).

4. Wes Haystead, *The 3,000-Year-Old Guide to Parenting* (Ventura, Calif.: Regal, 1991), 95.

5. Zig Ziglar, *Raising Positive Kids in a Negative World* (New York: Ballantine, 1989), 42, 50.

6. Stephen Covey, *The Seven Habits of Highly Effective People* (New York: Simon & Schuster, 1989), 32.

7. Tim Smith, *Eight Habits of an Effective Youth Worker* (Wheaton, Ill.: Victor, 1995), 15.

8. Exodus 20:12; NIV.
9. Denis Waitley, *Being the Best* (New York: Simon & Schuster, 1987), 55, 60.

Chapter 15: Becoming the Relaxed Parent

1. Wes Haystead, *The 3,000-Year-Old Guide to Parenting* (Ventura, Calif.: Regal, 1991), 247.
2. Merton and Irene Strommen, *Five Cries of Parents* (San Francisco: Harper & Row, 1985), 69.
3. Strommen, *Five Cries of Parents*, 95.
4. Ibid., 94–95.
5. Bruno Bettelheim, *A Good Enough Parent* (New York: Knopf, 1987), 333.
6. Proverbs 24:3–4; NIV.
7. Denis Waitley, *Being the Best* (New York: Simon & Schuster, 1987), 247.

In addition to Tim Smith's writing, he regularly conducts a weekend parenting conference entitled *The Relaxed Parent*. The usual format is Friday evening from 7:00–9:00 and Saturday 9:00 AM–2:30 PM.

For information regarding these conferences, please contact:

Wordsmith Communications
P.O. Box 7736
Thousand Oaks, CA 91359–7736
E-mail: tdwrdsmith@aol.com

If you are interested in information
about other books written from a
biblical perspective, please write
to the following address:

Northfield Publishing
215 West Locust Street
Chicago, IL 60610